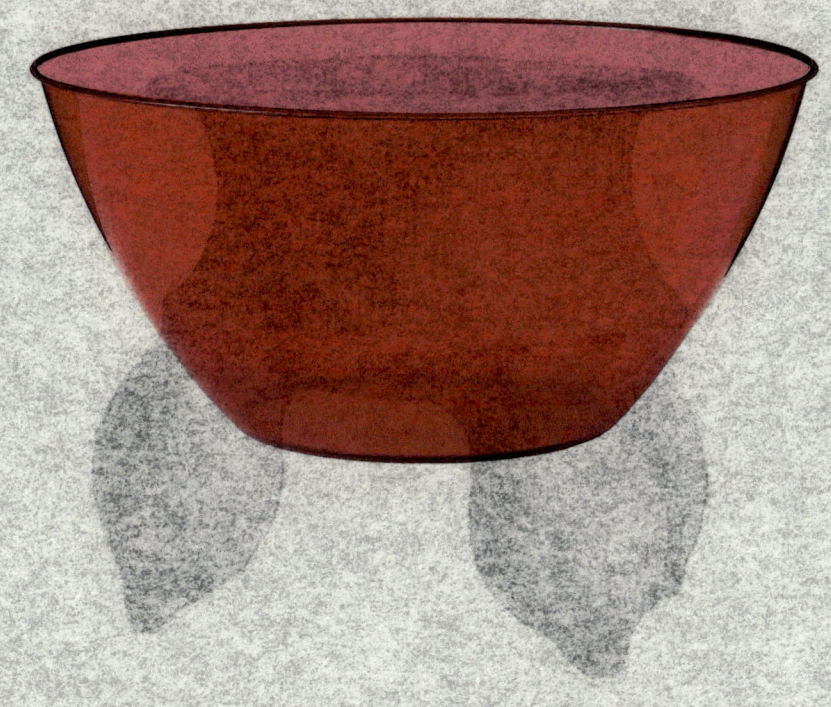

O plastic
Where are you from? Who are you?

And what explains your rare qualities?
So what are you doing?
Where did you come from? Starting from an object
Find his ancestors!*

And what explains your rare qualities?
So what are you doing?
Where did you come from? Starting from an object
Find his ancestors*

Dear Reader,

You enter a conversation about substance, about soil and its composition, about elements that bind with Fire and create new inorganic intelligence. This soil, this Earth, this body is made of many ideas, many thoughts that merge into a solid mass. Say this body is tortured, yet its spirit is fierce and we can feel it rage against the violence. This life offers an unconditional embrace of all there is.

El Plástico, the Sun that lives inside the Rock is an investigation into the evolution of material plasticity, a story about plastic whose native land is Mesoamerica. We want to think about plastic, and we want to understand the world through this natural phenomena, the glue, the binder, the creator and the annihilator. During a four year period (2014 to 2018), we made multiple research trips across the many states of Mexico and encountered individuals who generously shared their knowledge on or explained their relationship to plastic. From a weaver from Oaxaca, a sociologist working on trash collection in Mexico City to friends and chatty taxi drivers, we were encouraged to follow our enquiry around plastic even though it was not clear in the beginning where it was all heading. The photo documentation gathered in this book, is a personal diary and form of visual poetry that speaks of our ritual meditation on the subject.

We ask ourselves, what is common intelligence? Can the intelligence of a rock be regarded as having equal prodigy to life itself? Is it possible to hear the conversation between plastic and this rock, and follow its storyline?

With this work we have taken a detour from the usual guilt driven Anthropocentric reading of plastic, and rather see it as an integral part of the cause and effect that life on Earth exposes us to. For us, it is more interesting to speculate on where it all began. We no longer want to live inside the corpse of capitalism[†], we want to find refuge in the imaginary, in the possibility of telling stories that do not have a clear beginning or end. We want to leave the kettle boiling, take what's healing and leave the rest to evaporate in time and space.

Nida, 30 July 2019
Goda, Viktorija

Le Monde diplomatique, Mike Huguenor in conversation with Franco Berardo Bifo, July 2019.

A Plastics Tale
Goda Budvytytė, Viktorija Rybakova

Where There Is No Form, There Is a Norm
Catherine Malabou in conversation with Kristupas Sabolius

Mexican diary 2014–2018

Plastic Timeline (insert)

Workshop with students at the Universidad Nacional Autónoma de México in Morelia

A ritual in Zipolite beach in January 2018

The Sun that lives inside the Rock at Kunstverein München
Post Brothers
Chris Fitzpatrick

A Plastics Tale
Goda Budvytytė, Viktorija Rybakova

This timeline comprises a selection of notes and observations gathered in an attempt to trace how plasticity—found in the Earth's crust (rocks, soil) and other organic materials (trees, plants)—was, in Mesoamerica, being continuously improved by synthesising new natural materials; how the world eventually turned natural plastics into synthetically reproducible ones and how those components later returned to the sphere of geological resources in the form of plastiglomerate.

Miracle is always a sudden transformation of Nature.[1]
Roland Barthes

The timeline of this paper is divided into the following sub-categories: *Proto-plastics, Plastics, Synthetic plastics* and *Post-plastics*. All of these categories represent materials—natural or synthetic—that at earlier or later stages of their formation have been mouldable and in contact with human interest (hand) and production. In the category of *proto-plastics*, materials are included that come from natural geological resources, such as clay, metamorphic rock and amber. Clay and metamorphic rock or amber are very different in their solidity as we know them, but metamorphic rock and amber were once a plastic mass, and so they enter the chart before turning solid. In this chart, *Plastics* represent the first natural plastic materials produced by the Mesoamerican peoples by ways of synthesising natural components as early as 1600 BC. A mere 3,500 years later, Goodyear went on to discover the same process of vulcanisation, paving the way for the production of *Synthetic plastics* as we know today. *Post-plastics* is a melting pot of all plastics (presented in this timeline), which together form new consistencies. It is a new plastic material that contains a thorough memory of the history of Earth and humankind while at the same time is marked out as a distinctly new one. Post-plastic is abundant and nonlocal[2], it does not ask to be acknowledged and returns to the Earth as a material that has never been detached.

Inevitably, this geological timeline is also a personal one. It started as a collaborative endeavour, whereby we tried to unearth other ways of working together by stimulating one another's curiosity and looking for different models of knowledge production.

Paper
pulp
cellulose
polymers

Letters
ink
oil
polymers

If you break it down, that's where it all connects.
And matter morphs.

Proto-plastics

Human beings are attracted to telluric formations—minerals, patterns and colours—the solidity of Earth's labour. It is as if the Earth transcends its creative power to humans and a civilisation is born. Clay is one of the oldest building materials on Earth. When a human places their hands into clay, into a material that they can continue to

mould, they are replicating metamorphic processes taking place miles under the Earth's skin, eventually replacing the living shapes of nature into man-made objects. Turning from soft to hard, from amorphous to shaped, humankind also turns its gaze from one material to the next, looking for alternative materials.

Today, metamorphic rock forms 12% of the Earth's crust. It arrived on this planet without prior acknowledgment. Metamorphic rock is born in the deep layers of the Earth's strata, where it is exposed to high pressures and temperatures. Its molecules and atoms rearrange themselves from one consistency to another. Even if it becomes hard and solid at the end of the transformation process, it still holds the memory of having once been liquid. By acknowledging the process of its formation, which is significantly similar to the production of synthetic plastics in an industrial setting, it would appear evident that metamorphic rock can be considered a predecessor of plastic.

In the same way that metamorphic rock falls under the category of plastic, amber—once a soft, sticky tree sap, turned into a precious gemstone—is, in this timeline, considered as a plastic material too. It finds its way from the sea basin into daylight, where it continues to be reshaped and sculpted in the hands of humankind, who then return it to the Gods of their imagination.

Plastics

According to Michael J. Tarkanian and Dorothy Hosler, researchers in the earliest production of plastic, ancient Mesoamericans discovered the process of vulcanisation as early as 1600 BC by combining latex from Castilla elastica trees with the juice of the morning glory species Ipomoea alba. Pre-Hispanic Aztecs noted a variety of properties in those plants, which were commonly used for medicinal purposes. From this we can deduce that ethnopharmaceutical knowledge—the human curiosity to understand nature's processes on a molecular scale—led to a further synthesis that produced the first chemical mixture known as plastic today. It is interesting to observe that the morning glory flower, known as Convolvo in Latin, translates as "being interlaced". Considering that chemistry happens when atoms bind together, morning glory seems to embody it within its etymological root. Conveniently enough, in the wild, morning glory vines grow around the Castilla elastica tree, leaving little doubt that the two embrace each other in order to produce rubber.

The latex from C. elastica is a sticky, viscous white liquid when gathered directly from the tree, turning brown and becoming rigid, and brittle as it dries. When synthesised with I. alba juice, on the contrary, the material turns black and gains elasticity. The inversion of colour is also proof of the synthesis between the two substances—a process which was consciously performed. The

Mesoamericans did not only master the production process, they also experimented with the proportions of I.alba juice and C. elastica latex necessary to achieve different levels of consistency and elasticity of rubber. By alternating the consistency, Mesoamericans were able to produce different types of objects, such as rubber balls, shoe soles and joints for tools.

As a footnote to their research into rubber processing, Michael J. Tarkanian and Dorothy Hosler mention that when the Spanish conquistadores arrived in the lands of Mexico and other Americas in the sixteenth century and were first exposed to the material of rubber, and its elastic and bouncing properties, they lacked the vocabulary to describe it. Before that, rubber-bearing trees, as in the case of C. elastica, were unique to a particular region in the same way that the properties of elasticity were distinct to the bouncing balls produced by the Aztecs. Since materials with such properties were not a commodity in Europe, the concept of elasticity may have only entered the European psyche upon being exposed to this new material. To this day, the Spanish word for rubber remains *hule*, adopted from the Nahuatl[3] *ulli* or *olli*[4].

Aside from the latex of C. elastica, natural rubber can be produced from the Para rubber tree (Hevea brasiliensis), Guayule plant and Kazakh dandelion (Taraxacum kok-saghyz). In the Soviet Union, between 1931 and 1950, and in a few other countries during World War II, Taraxacum kok-saghyz was cultivated on a large scale as an emergency source of rubber when supplies of rubber from Hevea brasiliensis in Southeast Asia were under threat.

With the world economy changing and prices rising for synthetically produced rubber (produced from fossils), a new demand emerged to produce rubber out of naturally sourced materials. The interest in natural production is not only economic—naturally produced rubber is a lot more resilient in comparison to synthetic rubber.

Synthetic Plastics

It took more than three millenniums for Western culture to discover vulcanisation and how cross-linked polymers could combine into one supermolecule, to transform liquid rubber into a new material. The discovery can be pinpointed to 1839 when Charles Goodyear produced rubber from the Brazilian tree sap and sulphur, that occurred naturally in volcanic areas. The mixture was exposed to a heating process which led to the vulcanisation and subsequent material transformation from gummy and sticky to tough and durable, while withstanding the temperature changes. Only a dozen years after Goodyear's rediscovery, following the Brazilian rubber tree's (Hevea brasiliensis) decimation as a result of leaf blight, the American botanist J.M. Bigelow rediscovered the guayule plant. The same guayule that was used as a substitute to the Castilla elastica tree in the Classic Mesoamerican period. Thus the loop of history repeats.

In the consequent rush for the milky sap derived from Amazonian rubber trees and with the reintroduction of the vulcanisation process, demand for the material grew so quickly that for a short time in 1860 it exceeded the price of silver. The range of object typology increased as well. People began to put this new, waterproof, thermally and electrically resistant, semi-rigid material to use in various aspects of daily life, both intimate and public. Wheels for vehicles, pencil erasers, coating for hot air balloons, bladders for footballs, medical gloves, cables, waterproof clothes and shoes, and condoms are just a few of the objects that serve to connect, protect, prevent, inflate, wear and allow us to come into contact with substances that affect organisms. In short, rubber became a material that could make anyone an inventor; its leaky and viscous substance allowed the mind to unfold in many creative ways.

Following the success of rubber derived from tree sap, inventors looked into the possibility of a naturally occurring alternative that could be moulded into another plastic material. In 1854 shellac was introduced in the form of a thermodynamic plastic that can become as hard as rock when mixed with wood cellulose. Shellac itself is the secretion of female lac insects that suck tree sap and secrete the sap in the form of a bioadhesive polymer that can later be applied as a varnish or converted into hard plastic. When heated it is soft and flows under pressure but at room temperature it becomes rigid. This natural thermoplastic was used for making "union cases", protective frames for early forms of photographs kept under glass, such as daguerreotypes and ambrotypes.

Cellulose—the main ingredient that shapes the liquid mass—is a natural polymer found within the walls of plant cells that enables plants to remain robust and durable. It is obtained from wood pulp or the short fibres that adhere to cotton seeds. Cellulose lays the foundation for the further development of synthetic materials. As we move forward in the timeline of plastic, we will see how cellulose fibres were replaced by petrol-based fibres that are cheaper to exploit but are extremely harmful to the environment.

Around the same time that shellac was introduced as a thermoplastic[5], parkesine or polymer-named cellulose nitrate entered the scene as a soft, transparent, inflammable plastic. The chemical formula of parkesine marked the birth of mass domestic plastic production and was considered the first synthetically produced plastic. The main plasticiser element, that gives the plastic a smooth waxy appearance, is camphor—a crystalline compound that is distilled from the leaves and wood of the camphor laurel tree and used as a solvent that softens the rigid cellulose. Therefore, as a synthetic material, its main use was to imitate natural materials that were much harder to source and more expensive to produce things with—ivory, coral, amber, mineral stones, seashell and tortoiseshell—anything that attracts the human eye and fulfils demanding desires. Cellulose, when exposed to large quantities of nitric acid, which is chemically manufactured from naturally occurring ammonia found in volcanic areas, rainwater, animal and vegetable matter, is known as gunpowder; a highly explosive material.

At this point in time (at the end of the nineteenth century), human industries were still exploring the potential of natural materials and simple chemical reactions that gather homogeneous monomers into polymer chains. Subsequently, natural polymers like casein (milk protein), shellac and cellulose underwent polymerisation[6] processes and were transformed into thermoplastics. Up to this point, plastic was produced from raw materials, taken from the Earth and the process was not informed by the production of artificial mass. But the faster engines propelled, the more possibilities opened up to those industries driven by the petroleum business. Thus, a new chapter opened up on the propagation of petroleum, also known as "rock oil" and natural gas used to produce substances containing carcinogens, which disrupt the cellular metabolism of living organisms. Substances taken from the deep beneath the earth allow a polymer to last longer, resist even the hardest conditions and, in some cases, provide immortal life to the material.

In search for a shellac substitute, the Belgian chemist Leo Baekeland produced a hard, mouldable material, called Bakelite. This material, which was also pioneered as an early synthetic plastic, was made out of wood flour impregnated with synthetic resin; when heated and pressed, it was flexible enough to take any amorphous shape. Bakelite is considered to be the first synthetic thermosetting[7] plastic. The two organic and ultra-toxic compounds used to produce Bakelite are phenol and formaldehyde. Phenol is produced from petroleum and adds to the massive propagation of petroleum and black carbon deposition on the outmost surface of our planet, in turn causing pollution and global warming.

Formaldehyde is an evil substance that occurs naturally in coal and wood smoke and as an outdoor air pollutant in large cities. Furthermore, in search of a material of absolute desirable physical properties, Baekeland, who was interested in how plastic could be used in the construction business, experimented with asbestos silicate minerals to reinforce the material. The experiment ended up a commercial success, but triggered a whole other chain of toxicity in the environment. The good news is that Bakelite, a woody polymer, which is made of organic compounds, can be degraded by the white rot fungus Phanerochaete chrysosporium. It seems like nature will always have its own chemical formula to digest information fabricated by the drive of capitalism.

While Western polymer scientists were experimenting with hard plastics synthesised from plants, rubber production was steadily growing and, less than a century later, there was a clear demand for synthetic rubber—a superpolymer that would be produced in a lab and would not require transportation expenses or the complexities of dealing with global trade routes. Neoprene, invented by Wallace

Carothers in 1935, marked the beginning of the artificial propagation of carbon atoms. Vulcanisation became not merely an exposure to heat, but a highly polluting action that would create a new form of vulnerability for life. Ironically, as well as logically, Carothers was commissioned by the DuPont company that originally pioneered the production of gunpowder. It is important to mention that the DuPont company was also implicated in nuclear research (the Manhattan Project) for the first atomic bomb. Fire, sent from the Gods, rubber, obtained from sacred forests, wars, created by politics, and plastic—all of it was embraced at once.

Less than a century later, most of the natural plastics had been largely forgotten due to their complicated production processes, lesser durability, resistance to natural causes as well as the timely process of obtaining the raw material. Time shows us that plastic, as an idea of synthetic material, became an active political agent in the first part of the twentieth century. While the Western world is preoccupied by national capital and cultural influence, in the countries that are rich with natural and human resources, plastic moves into labs governed by politicians and oriented towards a military programme and political world divisions. The West invests in polymer research led by a drive to experiment with new materials that could be applied to a rapidly increasing production of warfare.

As mentioned earlier, rubber, the early offspring of plastic, plays a significant role in economic exchange and even competed with precious metals like silver, which is very well known for its use as a currency. Today, most of the plastics we buy are based on synthetic polymers and fuelled by petroleum, keeping the capital of oil companies safe. Recycling was introduced in the 1970s and since then plastic is being used as a non-monetary currency. In a country like Mexico, where we conducted our research, this exchange has become vital for city populations, where, according to sociological research, 70% of people work in black markets. Plastic plays a huge role in the black market business, especially that of trash collection. There is a whole chain of business that starts with street scavengers and ends up in the plastic factory, at the plastic moulding machine, which later returns to the black market in the form of a broom or a cup. Soft plastics and thermoplastics are all available for recycling; therefore, there seem to be endless possibilities to cash the whole labour process that plastic underwent before becoming an anonymous shape. There is an obvious end to petroleum-based production. It won't remain the cheapest method of undertaking mass production for long. Who knows, perhaps we are returning to simple primeval techniques—turning dandelion or milk into hard industrial materials—or just returning to a slower speed of life.

Post-plastics

The story of synthetic plastic begins with simple witchcraft—mixing substances derived from Amazonian plants—and ends up in a network of huge economic bubbles—beginning with the petroleum business and ending up in wallets, in the form of bank cards and bank notes.

To conclude our thoughts, we would like to analyse the data found in the records of industrial plastic development and trace the transformation process which brought plastic material onto the surface of our planet in the shape of a future fossil that slowly morphs with telluric matter and firmly assures us that it is here to stay.

Indeed, it is not clear how to befriend this action. It would require all possible human and non-human resources to subvert and destroy this vicious substance. Like a ghost, a rock, a freaky monomer chain that could be digested only by paraterrestrial microbes living in the deep seas or landing on our planet with galactic dust from space rockets. It is hauntingly expanding from micro to macro levels.

Son of Mother Earth
aka Metamorphic rock
didn't know back in 1800 BCE
that he would have a
synthetic brother
from an artificial mother
called–
plas–ti–glo–me–ra–te

In 2006, oceanographer Charles Moore discovered plastiglomerate— a new geological layer—a union of plastic and natural sediments. At first it was proclaimed that plastiglomerate was formed out of pieces of plastic (mostly PVC parts) floating on the surface of the Atlantic Ocean which had melted from exposure to the heat of the sun and eventually mixed with the sedimentary rock and other sediments on the shores of Hawaii. A long and smooth collaboration between different forces of nature and human presence. Eventually, it was proven that plastiglomerate, which at first glance looks like a mineral, was actually formed in the conditions of a campfire accident. Again, the element of Fire remains an essential component in plastic's history as the creator of a new Nature. It destroys and creates space for the other.

Recently, a new plastic manufacturing process, Mnemosynation, was developed. It was named after the Greek goddess of memory, Mnemosyne. As a process, it allows plastic to change its shape or return to its primary polymer network architecture—turning from stable to biodegradable, from soft to hard or from elastic to rigid—when it is triggered by an external stimulus, such as UV light or heat. The heating of shape-memory polymers activates their

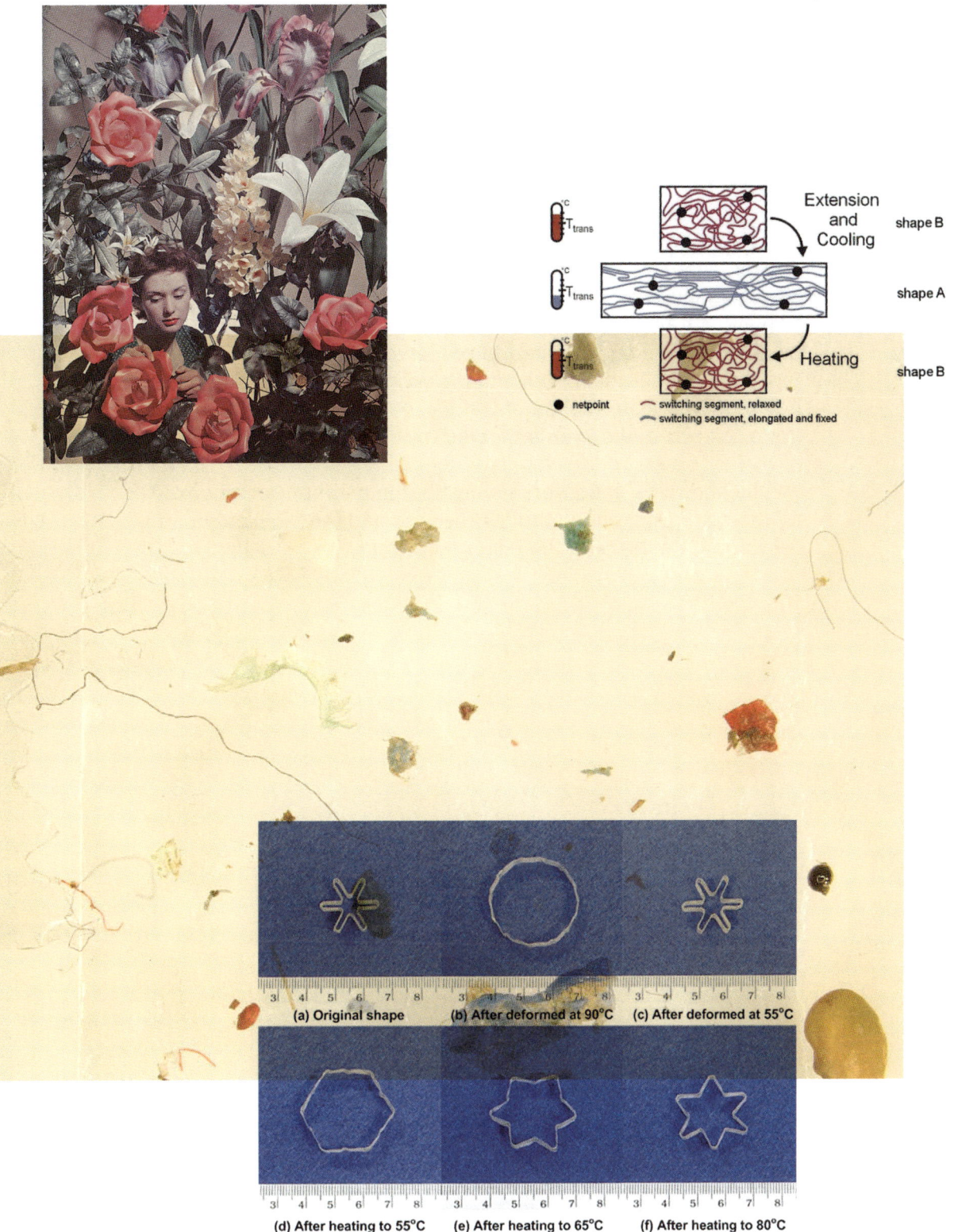

shape B
shape A
shape B

- netpoint
- switching segment, relaxed
- switching segment, elongated and fixed

(a) Original shape   (b) After deformed at 90°C   (c) After deformed at 55°C

(d) After heating to 55°C   (e) After heating to 65°C   (f) After heating to 80°C

"memory." This material finds its place in bodies that need to be repaired and that are in need of prolonging their techno life.

Plastic enters the human body in the form of a heart valve or an artificial blood vessel; mistaken for a jellyfish, it remains in the guts of marine animals or, buried on the sea bed, it preserves itself and becomes a part of the deep ocean's ecology. In the same way that a rock's chemical information is affected by the environment, e.g., by the level of salt in the sea, marine animals and the information of their bodies, plastic is being affected and befriended as a matter that can transform into something else. There is no finitude to things, merely because they are never single.

The fact that plastic can be viewed as a memory container fascinates our imagination and we would like to believe that the material came to being not only as a destructive force against Nature, but rather as an observing one, created to preserve the history of different types of natures—that of a human, a cyborg or an insect. If a miracle is a sudden transformation of Nature (!) (?), then plastic could be the black box of the events that led to this transformation.

Plastic and rock—in conversation with one another—are shocked by the comfort of each other's presence and the familiarity of the fiery affair that brought them into this world.

Notes

1. Barthes, 1990: 110.
2. Morton, 2013: 1.
3. Nahuatl, known historically as Aztec, is a language or group of languages of the Uto-Aztecan language family.
4. Michael J. Tarkanian and Dorothy Hosler, "America's First Polymer Scientists: Rubber Processing, Use, and Transport", in Latin American Antiquity, Vol. 22, No. 4 (December 2011) (Society for American Archaeology, http://www.jstor.org/stable/23072570), pp. 469–486.
5. Thermoplastics, on the other hand, remain soft after they cool. They can be remoulded and changed and are the plastics that we are most familiar with e.g. water bottles, bags etc. Thermoplastics include polyethylene and polypropylene. The ability of these plastics to be remoulded is what makes them so useful. They can be manufactured in one place (as pellets) and then shipped elsewhere to be remoulded into a product of just about any shape.
6. The process of polymer molecules forming into a three-dimensional network is called polymerisation.
7. Thermoset-plastics, after being heated and shaped, are cooled and become very hard. They cannot return to their original form and are generally very hard. These are the plastics can be found in car parts or aeroplanes and include things like polyesters, polyurethanes, and epoxies. http://www.petroleum.co.uk/plastic-production

References

Aisha, P. Nasreen, J, Wadud, A., Tanwir, A. 2013. Methods of processing of Lac (Laccifer lacca Kerr) described in Unani system of Medicine, *Research Journal of Pharmaceutical Sciences*, Vol. 2(8), September, p. 5–7.

Backhaus, R. A. 1985. Rubber Formation in Plants—A Mini-Review, *Israel Journal of Botany*, Vol.34, p. 283–293

Barcena, M. 1876. "The Rocks Known ad Mexican Onyx", in *Proceedings of the Academy of Natural Sciences of Philadelphia*, Vol. 28, Academy of Natural Sciences, pp. 166–168. Available at: http://www.jstor.org/stable/4060011.

Bathes, R. 1990. "Plastics", in *The plastics age: from modernity to post-modernity*, ed. Penny Sparke, Victoria & Albert Museum: London

Berthier, H. C. 2003. *Garbage, Work And Society*. UNAM Institute for Social Research.

Beilen, J. B. van, Poirier, Y. 2007. Guayule and Russian Dandelion as Alternative Sources of Natural Rubber, *Critical Reviews in Biotechnology*, p. 217–23.

Caillois, R. 1985. *The Writing of Stones*. Charlottesville: University Press of Virginia.

Corcoran, P. L., Moore, Ch. J., Jazvac, K. 2014. *Plastiglomerate*, An anthropogenic marker horizon in the future rock record, *GSA Today*, vol. 24, no. 6, p. 4–8.

Gould, H. 2015. The journey towards more sustainable rubber leads to Russian dandelions, *The Guardian*, 6 November 2015. Available at: https://www.theguardian.com/sustainable-business/2015/nov/06/rubber-tyres-russian-dandelions-sustainability-timberland-shoes-waste.

Lloyd, F. E. 1942. *Guayule: A Rubber-Plant Of The Chihuahuan Desert*, J.a. Lippincott Company.

Morton, T. 2013. *Hyperobjects, Philosophy and Ecology after the End of the World*, Minnesota: University of Minnesota Press.

Pereda-Miranda, R., Rosas-Ramırez, D. Castaneda-Gomez, J. 2010. Resin Glycosides from the Morning Glory Family, *Progress in the Chemistry of Organic Natural Products*, Vol. 92, ed. Kinghorn, A.D.; Falk, H.; Kobayashi, J. Available at: http://www.springer.com/978-3-211-99660-7

Preciado, B. 2003. *Testo junkie: sex, drugs, and biopolitics in the pharmacopornographic era*. New York: Feminist Press

Tarkanian, M. J., Hosler, D. 2011. America's First Polymer Scientists: Rubber Processing, Use, and Transport, *Latin American Antiquity*, Society for American Archaeology, Vol. 22, No. 4, December 2011, pp. 469–486. Available at: http://www.jstor.org/stable/23072570.

Villagran, L. 2012. Garbage for Future. As Mexico City Modernizes, A Debate Emerges: Who Owns the Trash? *Next American City*, Vol. 1, Issue 14. Available at: https://nextcity.org/features/view/garbage-for-the-future.

Links

Cellulose, CAMEO: Conservation & Art Materials Encyclopedia Online. Available at: http://cameo.mfa.org/wiki/Cellulose

Cellulose Acetate, Interplex India Private Limited. Available at: http://www.interplexindia.com/aca.htm

Cellulose Acetate, CAMEO: Conservation & Art Materials Encyclopedia Online. Available at: http://cameo.mfa.org/wiki/Cellulose_acetate

Clay, The Free Encyclopaedia Wikipedia. Available at: *https://en.wikipedia.org/wiki/Clay*. [Retrieved: 7 March 2017].

Du Pont, The Free Encyclopedia Wikipedia. Available at: https://en.wikipedia.org/wiki/DuPont.

General Characteristics of Polymers, Conservation and Art Materials Encyclopedia Online, Museum of Fine Arts, Boston, 2007. Available at: http://cameo.mfa.org/images/9/97/Download_file_333.pdf

Gutta-percha or Thermoplastic Union Cases? Old Photographic Online Vintage Photography Magazine. Available at: http://oldphotographic.com/tips/gutta-percha-or-thermoplastic-union-cases

Metamorphic rock, The Free Encyclopaedia Wikipedia. Available at: https://en.wikipedia.org/wiki/Metamorphic_rock. [Retrieved: 7 March 2017].

Mnemosynation. Available at: http://www.liquisearch.com/shape-memory_polymer/applications/potential_industrial_applications

Neoprene, CAMEO: Conservation & Art Materials Encyclopedia Online. Available at: http://cameo.mfa.org/wiki/Neoprene

Neoprene, The Free Encyclopedia Wikipedia. Available at: https://en.wikipedia.org/wiki/Neoprene

Nitrocellulose, The Editors of Encyclopædia Britannica. Available at: https://www.britannica.com/science/nitrocellulose, 2010

Parkesine, The Free Encyclopedia. Available at: Wikipedia https://en.wikipedia.org/wiki/Parkesine, 2016

Parkesine, History of Plastic. Available at: http://www.historyofplastic.com/plastic-history/history-of-plastics/

Parkesine, CAMEO: Conservation & Art Materials Encyclopedia *Online*. Available at: http://cameo.mfa.org/wiki/Parkesine

White rot fungus, The Free Encyclopedia Wikipedia. Available at: https://en.wikipedia.org/wiki/Phanerochaete, 2016

Where There Is No Form, There Is a Norm
Catherine Malabou in conversation with
Kristupas Sabolius

What happens when symbolic and biological meet up? How can mental and material resonate? What is the transition from synaptic to cultural and vice versa? Or rather, what does it mean for us—plastic beings—to arrive at a point where we try to understand the history of the plastics?

Catherine Malabou, an important and imaginative voice in contemporary philosophy, likes to refer to historian Dipesh Chakrabarty, who claims that the acceptance of the Anthropocene generates a kind of mental problem. It is impossible to conceive of ourselves as a geological force without producing a new form of consciousness that generates a break in reflexivity.

More precisely, what is at stake in the dialectics between plasticity and plastics? As many of us are very well aware, Malabou is famous for developing her signature philosophical concept—plasticity—which she draws from her reading of Hegel and which, affected by her search of the fantastic in Heidegger, has been constantly expanded and re-contextualised, even in the realm of neuroscience and epigenetics. It is played out through the famous triple meaning, which designates both an ability to receive, to give and to destroy form.

And it is namely the odd and untraditional third meaning that could be found at the core of the fate of plastics. Although famous for their indestructibility, polymers are treated as prime polluters and the nemesis of ecology, namely because of the same reason they bring forward the question of death. As Malabou puts it during our discussion, "ecological thinking will always have to deal with death and destruction—to think that one day we can eliminate destruction is impossible". The plastic meaning of plastics encompasses both decay and immortality. As long as they resist death, they spread death. The true question of ecology regards the inelegant ways of remaining alive; whereas, by becoming plastic, we have to learn dying again.

However, "I have no definition of plasticity" she confesses at the very beginning of our conversation. And this recognition of the incapacity to define the fundamental idea that she has been elaborating on for decades is anything but a figure of speech. Plasticity represents and attempts to think through, with and along dynamics of change, that induces into transformation both the thinker and what is thought.

Maybe that is the reason why Malabou proposed to conceive plasticity as the "motor scheme", the imaginative power to activate thinking by producing an image that delineates the trajectory of thinking while at the same time granting it an aspect of indeterminacy and incompleteness. By aiming to philosophise mutability one cannot rely on rigid structures; one should express a readiness to become plastic as well.

It is not an easy task to avoid reductions and simplifications in order to make room for a dialectical encounter. As she put it in *Plasticity at the Dusk of Writing*, "the scheme declines historically in so many figural ways through which being and meaning are announced to themselves, as much in the purity of a thought as in the materiality of a culture".

So what fuels this motor scheme in light of today's challenges? We sat together to discuss the present and future of plasticity.

KRISTUPAS SABOLIUS Let's start from a traditional, or even boring question regarding the concept of "plasticity" that you proposed and elaborated on over the course of several decades. It is well-known that you find this notion both in Hegel and neuroscience. However, the first book of yours that I read was *The Heidegger Change. On the Fantastic in Philosophy*. And you show that Heidegger does not use the word plasticity, he is rather talking about change, transformation and metamorphosis. The same is also true for Derrida. However, both of them appear to be "plastic" in your vision of philosophy. Every time you engage with a certain author or domain of knowledge, you add something to the concept, as you put it, in order "to elaborate the concept". Thus, the concept itself is plastic, as if it were the plasticity of plasticity…

CATHERINE MALABOU Absolutely.

KS So within that trajectory of transformation, after having done all this work, what is plasticity for you today?

CM What is plasticity today? I think you are right to say that my plasticity is plastic itself, meaning that it changes all the time, shifts directions, etc. But if I can say a few words before arriving at today's moment, I would say that the philosophers I was interested in as a student were mainly Derrida and Heidegger, and also Hegel. And I tried to combine their philosophies, because there was little chance of working with Derrida, especially writing something like a PhD on Hegel, and hoping that it could lead somewhere.

And I discovered that Heidegger's and Derrida's visions of metaphysics were those of philosophical tradition that was able to immanently change, both because something was repressed in them (like Being, for Heidegger), and also because of their historicity. So, I thought that maybe I could interrogate this immanent mutability of philosophy and, perhaps, use it against Heidegger and Derrida to show that it was something in Hegel that he pointed at this mutability that they hadn't seen.

Thus, plasticity for me, from very early on, became a general movement of changeability as philosophy—like tradition is always multiple, there is something repressed in it. I conceived plasticity both as a general principle of change, and as a concept within this movement; so, both as a whole, and as its parts.

Each time I work on a new issue, like, for example recently, epigenetics, I always look at both directions at the same time. What is this historical movement that brought me to think of that problem today, where is this immanence, mutability of history that brought me to think of this problem? But, at the same time, trying to grasp this general movement, i.e. see where the concept of plasticity is. For instance, the general context of my work with epigenetics was this discussion with Meillassoux and new realisms, whereas the concept of plasticity was epigenetics itself. I guess it is always a network between a general movement and a network of neurons.

Where am I today? Today I am working on the philosophy of anarchism, I develop this concept of anarchy, trying to show that this concept of anarchy has been repressed all along the twentieth century in philosophy, and at the same time very present, like in Levinas for example.

I am trying now to move towards politics and see how my general frame—mutability and the neuron inside of mutability—is applicable to politics through this concept of anarchy.

KS In *What Should We Do With Our Brain?* and *The New Wounded* you already provided some preliminary thoughts on the political role of the plastic. More recently, your engaged with Foucault and Agamben by criticising their idea of biopolitics and their concept of life which stems from it. You notice that they reject the scientific dimension, focusing only on the symbolic level, whereas your philosophical project is aiming to reconcile the realms of biological life and symbolical life. From what you are saying now, it seems that it also has something to do with a certain political philosophy. What is the political meaning of plasticity?

CM I aim to interpret the plasticity as anarchy—i.e. the absence of principle, the substitution of shaping and the ability to form principles—and to conceive anarchy as a mode of inventing one's own conditions of life, one's own social conditions, shaping one's own collective being without any kind of discipline from above, any form of party, any form of centralised command. And I am thinking about the ways Marxism can become relevant to address the discoveries of neuroscience.

I am engaging with the disappearance of the state, the reconstruction of the subject of politics. I am also thinking how to address the ecological questions in this context—from a horizontal level, so to say.

At the same I am interested in the question of post-anarchism that is inspired by Foucault and all the Occupy movements, seen in the light of so called "old anarchism", based on the ideas of Pierre-Joseph Proudhon, Piotr Kropotkin and others, as well as in relation to science and neurobiology. It is known that post-anarchism is very much against the scientific take. So it is a kind of dialectics that I am trying to elaborate between, let's say, traditional anarchism and new anarchism.

KS There is a book coming up?

CM I am working very hard at the moment. And I am teaching a course on this subject.

KS On a different note, I thought it would be worth highlighting the work of an artist duo named *laumes* (Goda Budvytytė and Viktorija Rybakova) who have been conducting artistic research into the origin of the plastics. They refer to Michael J. Tarkanian and Dorothy Hosler who claimed that plastics were discovered and produced by the Mesoamerican peoples by ways of synthesising natural components as early as 1600 BC. Pre-Hispanic Aztecs noted that the plants used in this synthesising process for medicinal purposes also had a variety of other notable properties. By alternating the consistency of the materials, Mesoamericans were able to produce different type of objects, such as rubber balls, shoe soles and joints for tools. The paradox is that for those indigenous people plastics constituted as a development of, "natural materials", so to say, whereas nowadays cross-linked polymers are seen as "artificial intruders" into the realm of nature. I think this reversal resonates with your thinking in that there is a plasticity not only of plasticity, but also of plastics as well. The plastics contain a history that is also plastic.

CM That is absolutely true. Moreover, this relates also to the history of chemical materials in general. There is a long history, from polymers to other synthetic materials.

KS And since you mentioned ecology and environmentalism among your recent interests (some time ago you also published an article on the question of the Anthropocene): what trajectory can the philosophy of plasticity open up in this context?

CM Certainly, this is a paradox: plastics are the enemies of ecology, so immediately we tend to think about indestructible plastics, and identify plastics with pollution. And this is very important—I am not trying to avoid this question in any way. My concept of plasticity, as you very well know, has always had a destructive dimension.

KS Yes, a famous third meaning.

CM Exactly. I don't share the views of naïve ecology by claiming that we just need to get rid of this and the problem will be solved. I think ecological thinking will always have to deal with death and destruction—to think that one day we can eliminate destruction is impossible. That is why plasticity is at the heart of this dilemma. On the one hand, it designates the threat of destruction—it is only one world and, in that sense, it is fragile and exposed to its own end; on the other hand, it means recycling, it means regenerating…

The paradox is that, only by becoming plastic ourselves, can we can deal with both of these two aspects. For instance, these two aspects of plasticity and technology you will find in Marshall McLuhan's writing, someone who is not that read anymore. I was rereading him again recently, and he is fascinating. McLuhan says that what liberates us simultaneously hypnotises us; he talks about this numbness of technology. And this exactly points to the risks of technology—we have to remain plastic, which is a kind of dynamic attitude, in order to address it; otherwise we are paralysed by it. In that sense, ecology is paralysing as well.

KS Ecology is paralysing in many senses. For instance, it produces a certain anesthetising effect in theories that try to approach the question of "anthropos" of the Anthropocene.

CM I agree with Dipesh Chakrabarty who says that the problem is the consciousness that is produced by the Anthropocene. Because, when we, as human beings, become a natural force—which is the meaning of the Anthropocene—how can we remain conscious of ourselves as a geological force? This breaks the reflexivity of consciousness.

When Chakrabarty addresses this question, he points out that we cannot think about the Anthropocene in terms of responsibility: you are not responsible, I am not responsible. Something else is going on.

KS There are discourses that propose to see the agency of geological force as the problem of capital, thus advocating for the term the Capitalocene.

CM This is also something I address through the question of anarchism. I am really tired of bringing everything back to capitalism. There are problems of power and domination that are not reducible to economic exploitation which, of course, remains undeniable. But to become aware of ourselves as a natural force, as I was just saying, allows a new problem emerge, that cannot be reducible to an economic issue.

KS Posthuman turn and the question of revenge. In your recent writings, you propose, through the Heideggerian reading of Nietzsche, to bring the concept of revenge to the centre of the problem of the human. I quote: "You can now guess what the problem is: are we able to deal with this new urgency of repetition without seeking revenge towards it? Are we able to repeat without seeking revenge? Without trying to crucify time and transiency, without trying to invent new forms of cruelty?" This way the defining factor in understanding the human turns out to be namely revenge—not culture, not language, not technology, but revenge. What is the future of the human, having in mind this possible reconsideration of revenge?

CM This reconsidering of revenge at the centre of the human has to do something important with the concept of plasticity. What I have in mind here is the idea of substitution or replacement. Of course, thinking on the overman, superhuman and figures like that, brings in the idea of substitution. Namely, who will replace the human, who will come next? And this can be a very fruitful discussion in the context of the posthuman or the transhuman (like augmented humanity, etc.). We should pose the question: what is the relationship between the technological augmentation of our capacities and revenge?

KS You were engaged in a discussion with Quentin Meillassoux, and this even led you to write a book on Kant. In light of current discussions on speculative realism and materialism, the revalorisation of the concept of the real occurred as one of the very important tendencies within the context of continental philosophy. You call yourself a materialist, but never a realist. Why is that? Are the concepts of reality / the real important for you?

CM First of all, I am not sure where the concept of the real in speculative realism comes from. I guess it primarily stems from analytical philosophy, more than anything else. What is interesting in their approach—and this is why I became curious about all of this discussion—is that I find the idea of the real that is absolutely indifferent to the subject very challenging. I guess this is what "literal" means for Meillassoux—not a metaphor, not a signification—because all this would imply a subjective and finite take.

I like this idea of the desert, of something that is perfectly autonomous (and even the word "autonomous" is affectively connoted already). Neutral, indifferent and raw—I think this is very interesting. And I do think all philosophical thinking has to confront itself with this hypothesis, because it also means that nothing exists. In a certain sense to say that "there is only the real" means "there is nothing". So, it is very close to the equivalent between the real and nothingness.

And I think, for Meillassoux, contingency means namely this possibility of total destructibility. And I reckon that this extreme negativity is the challenge of philosophy. We know different versions of this in ancient philosophy, for instance, scepticism etc. This is what I recognised in his book—a new version of this extreme challenge.

However, if we are coherent with this vision, we then have to wonder who this subject is—in this vision—because we are here as well. We also are real. And this is the question Meillassoux never addresses. Our own reality, as a residue of this real, is never interrogated.

And, I think, this is where materialism is absolutely indispensable. Materialism is the response of the subject to the real. Or, to be more exact, materialism is the reflection of the subject's own materiality in relation to the real. This is my problem with speculative realism. If the subject disappears, what becomes of it? It is also part of the real. Where is the reality of the subject? What is it?

KS I think the question of radical imagination (as elaborated by Cornelius Castoriadis)—as a certain response to and engagement with the material becomes a very important issue. The role of determination in the history of philosophy was to act as an essential and often implicit condition of logical thinking. It can be seen as a hyper-category that provides a foundation to all the laws of logic and metaphysics. According to him, every realism—and I would add that this is relevant also to a variety of its recent versions, including Meillassoux—cannot be established without a primordial presupposition: determining what is real. That is to say, every realism tends to be deterministic because of its drive to designate the limits of the real, even speculatively.

On the other hand, determinism seems to be part of the agenda of scientific reductivism. In your thoughts, you propagate the idea of the matter and of materialism that is not necessarily deterministic. Your attempt to put continental philosophy and biology or neuroscience into dialogue with one another expresses a need to open up.

I would formulate it as problem for radical imagination—how can we imagine ourselves as realists, notwithstanding the challenge of determination? Is it possible to be a scientist and escape determinism?

CM It is a very important question. I do think it is possible—as you know very well, it has been challenged by quantum physics and also philosophical work done by Karen Barad, whom I like very much. I find her book *Meeting the Universe Halfway*, which addresses this question in the context of Niels Bohr, very interesting. She takes determinism seriously, but at the same time works in a space that is very different from it.

Or, let's take neurology. We have some scientists who represent reductionist neurology, or, some people working in this indeterminate space, questioning the validity of boundaries. Plasticity namely appears to be at the core of this problem.

KS What possibilities are provided by plasticity as a non-deterministic concept? How would you outline the role of plasticity in opening-up scientific determinism?

CM I think this has to do with Meillassoux's main contradiction—to mention the field of transfinite and Cantor's mathematics, because this is the plasticity of the concept of infinity that he is talking about. Cantor's infinity is indetermined, it is absolutely not deterministic.

I think we could take many scientific fields and demonstrate that the main concepts are open. They are being elaborated in a not deterministic way.

The other problem is that scientists only take those philosophers who are really reductionists seriously. Even the realists, that we were talking about, such as Meillassoux, but also Harman, Brasier and others, are not taken seriously. You have to be from Oxford and tick certain boxes in order to be taken into consideration. And I don't have a solution here.

But what we can do, at the very least, is take science seriously. Because this was a big error of deconstruction philosophy and all these trends. We have to go to the conferences and try to engage with them. I do that myself. Do they listen to me? I don't know.

KS Do they listen to you?

CM Maybe they listen, but what they do with what they hear—I don't know. They sometimes react by saying "oh, your concept of plasticity is a metaphor". But, still, I consider it as the thing we have to do: it is important to exist; and to let them know that we exist. On the other hand, twenty years ago they used to think that philosophers were not on their side, or at least never engaged with them. I think this is changing now.

KS Do you see that as a thread that Continental philosophy needs to follow? I mean to look for a common ground between science and philosophy?

CM Oh, yes. Most certainly, I don't say it is the only way whatsoever. But, yes, definitely. There are so many important things going on, because it is impossible to remain outside of it.

KS And that's what you try to engage with in a discussion on neuroplasticity or epigenetics.

CM Unfortunately, there is a return of hard determinism. For example, in biology. I was very happy with epigenetics for its opening trajectories—but, in fact, it has been challenged in many ways, since there are a lot of opposite tendencies in how the discoveries of science are applied. For instance, the famous DNA test that allows you to trace your ancestors. It is terrible!

There are countries where people have to undergo this test; and if the results determine that a person is not 100% of a certain heritage, this person is not entitled to social security. It is used by certain countries as a means of discrimination. We are witnessing the return of eugenics: "look at me—I am 100% white" etc. It means not only rejecting the discoveries of epigenetics, but rejecting the idea that we are not totally determined, that there is a kind of plasticity in us that does not allow us to be reduced to our DNA, that environment is also very important, etc. This test (or, at least, the way it is used) is the negation of plasticity.

I read a lot about these tests—and they are completely challengeable, you can interpret them in very different ways. They give you clues, but no exact answers.

KS In this context—what is the role of philosophy today?

CM My vision is very simple. I think that our activity as philosophers is to open spaces—spaces of freedom, spaces of reading etc. We have to fight against all these forms of closure and borders. For example, one could have thought that genetic determinism is over, but here it is—the old devil back again.

KS On a different note—your investigation into the notion of plasticity constantly brings back the question of form; while being fully aware that it is a very metaphysical concept. For example, as you noted on some occasions, Derrida conceived the concept *eidos* or *morphè* as forever prisoner to metaphysics. We could recall Gilbert Simondon who tried to relinquish the hylomorphic ontology, by proposing his philosophy of individuation. However, you claim yourself to be a materialist, namely by elaborating the concept of form. As if by trying to maintain old metaphysical terminology, you propose an effort to transform it as well. Does it mean that we cannot think of ontology outside the form? Are humans dependent on the metaphysical necessity of forms?

CM Maybe this is a blind spot in my work. I honestly would not be able to give you a definition of what I mean by form. This is precisely what I don't know, this is my blind spot. But, at the same time, it is something I am very attached to. It is at the heart of what I am doing. What I can tell you—again in a very simple manner: where and when there is no form, there is a norm.

Ok, let's take form away. What would you find instead? For instance, in Deleuze you find the concept of play (*le jeu*), which means the rules, meaning, a certain type of norms. Or, if you consider Derrida there is something extremely rigid about the rule. You can play with it, but it comes back all the time—like the rule of deconstruction.

If you look at what form was substituted with in philosophy, you have a rule which has no flesh. And it is terrible. It means discipline. If you take a form away, you find a system in a terrible sense.

Conversely, take Hegel, for example. The concept of form is constantly present in his philosophy. The term "rule" never appears in his work. Dialectics is always about forms. This also pertains to the problem of the transcendental, which is also a kind form, although adamant. What saves Kant from being totalitarian, is namely his notion of form. Because a form can always be transformed. What about the rules?

KS You need to obey them.

CM Exactly, you need to obey them. Of course, you can play with them, but a rule is a rule. I prefer form.

Of course, form can be a rule. But there is always space for accidents, changes, like in Aristotle. Once again, I cannot tell you what the form is for me. But I know what it is not—it is not a rule.

KS Considering it along the lines of your work, maybe it is a metaphysical wound, we have to take seriously?

CM Absolutely. It is a wound. And wounds take their time in the process of healing, without obeying anything, except the general principles. But still, a certain autonomy is always maintained.

I think Foucault worked on this, in his final books, the ones that people usually don't read. And they are my favourite—they talk about transforming oneself, instead of just obeying some very good norms.

KS The readings of Hegel and Heidegger brought the concept of imagination into your thinking. I truly believe that, by proposing the creative dynamics of plasticity, you are one of the rare examples of contemporary philosophy that take the question of imagination seriously, as part of a philosophical stance. Would you agree with me calling you an "imaginary materialist" (as an alternative to "speculative realism")?

CM I have never thought of that. I did the class on the symbolic some time ago, where I went through the developments of the symbol, as well as the differences between image and symbol. This is great, but I have to think about it. We would need to elaborate on this further.

Mexican diary 2014–2018

During our walks we scanned the multifaceted surface of Mexico city with an unfocused gaze. The flow of life in this huge, crowded city took us by the hand and pulled us along. As Emanuele Coccia wrote, "Life as immersion is one in which our eyes are ears. To feel is always to touch, both oneself and the universe that surrounds us."

In this state of immersion, we noticed inescapably that with every corner turned, with every taco bought, with every monetary transaction, we were forever in touch with plastic. It's as if every person you meet and shake hands with is wearing rubber gloves!

Back then—
I was made from a stone

Found in the depths of the caves,
caressed gently by the warm hands
I took their shapes

Now I am a mould multiplied
millions of times, I carry
gluuuuue
and they call me PVC clay

One of the first stations we headed to to look for answers about the nativity of plastic was the National Museum of Anthropology in Mexico City. Clay bowls, jade relics for Mesoamerican Gods, sleeping mats made from palm fibres— all these goods were produced by human hands, the same hands that created the idea of a polymer that can take any shape today. Going deeper into the dark rooms of the museum, we see objects that silently carry spirits as old as the world itself and discover that some of them are carrying a strong visual resemblance to the contemporary objects that are mass-produced today.

The Sun that lives inside the rock
The hand, the rock,
The Fire when they touch

The shape was born from clay and hardened back
into the rock

The flower open as a gaping heart
Embraces a tree, becoming tree-like

The spell was brought back into the Earth

‡ Text on ullamaliztli from the National Museum of Anthropology in Mexico

Waltzing further across long museum corridors designed by Pedro Ramírez Vázquez, we finally meet with the object that caused a meaningful turn in our open proposition to search for the roots of plastic in Central America. A rubber ball produced in the low-lying tropical zones of Mexico by "rubber people", the Olmecs—the first product of vulcanisation; a process that enabled synthetic future as we know it. Rubber as a man-made material marks the first symptoms of plastic life, *ullamaliztli* (the Aztec word for ballgame) originates it in Mexico. In the image on the page opposite you can see evidence from the past—a ballplayer depicted in the Tepantitla murals that decorate the campus of the ancient city of Teotihuacan.

The ball game among Mexicas.

The peoples of ancient Mesoamerica practiced a ball game; a ritual sport that determined the dangers faced by the sun on its daily journey across the heavens, thus predicting its fate.

For the Mexicas, the sacred ball game was ullamalizli, *a word derived from rubber, the material used to make the ball, which was skillfully moved by the players, and possessed a precise bounce which surprised the European conquerors. The game was played on a special court called a* tlaxco, *which was a patio formed in a unique shape, similar to an "I" or double "T"; on either side there were slopes and walls where the stone rings,* tlaxtemalacatl, *were placed, one to the south and one to the north, through which the balls had to pass when struck either with the hips or forearm. The ends of the court, where the teams were located, were to the east and west.*

When a play was made that went against the movement of the sun, a decapitation was carried out, the blood shed vitalised the Earth and the Sun. Secular betting was one feature of the ball game in Mexico–Tenochtitlan.‡

When my creator
learned that anything
can become something
and that this endless transformation
is part of every cycle
I became a brush,
a bowl, a mirror frame
made out of trunk
or turtle shell,
an amber bracelet

"One is born with forces that one did not contrive. One lives by giving form to these forces. The forms one gets from the others.", *We Mortals*, Alphonso Lingis.

Can you trans(late) the form?

………………………………….

I embody shapes that lived before me
I learn and I transform

Disarming the effects of time
We circulate through one another

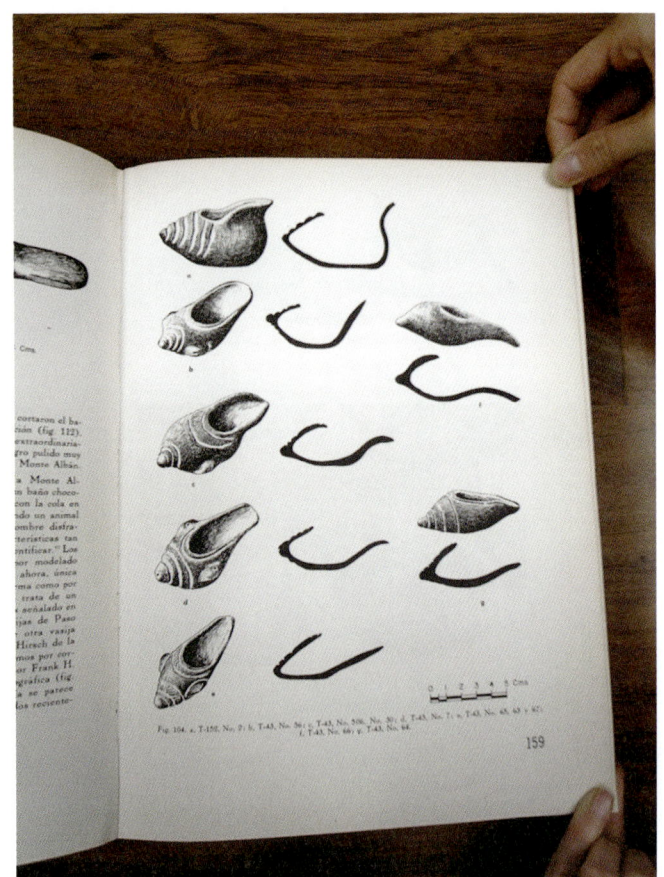 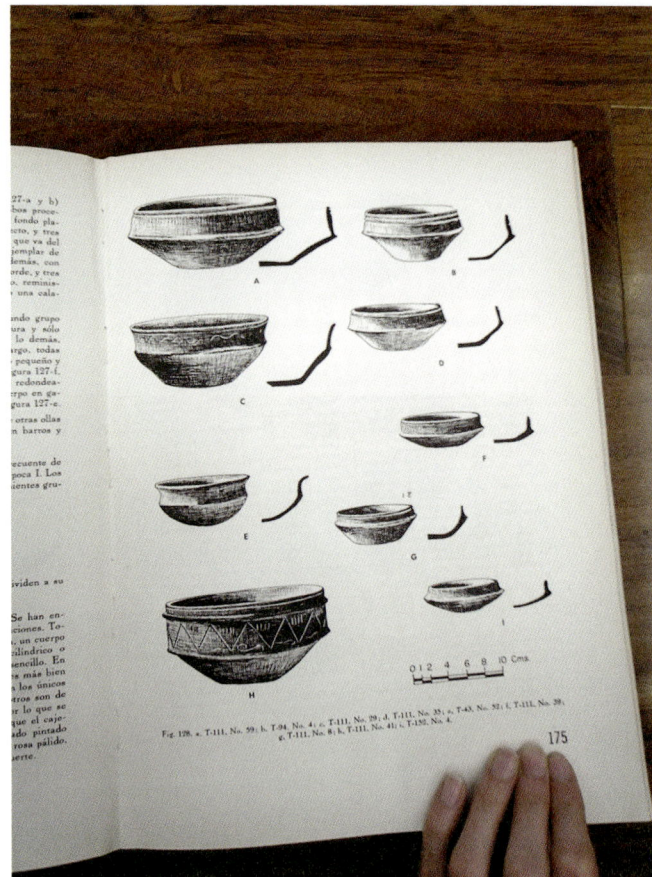

Microtopology charts of ceramic bowls found in the Monte Alban area, what is now the Mexican state of Oaxaca. Through the study of images at La Ciudadela (the Library of Mexico), we traced the origins of modern plastic salsa bowls that imitate the forms of their Oaxacan ancestors.

Fig. 133. a, T-43, No. 39; b, T-94, No. 8; c, T-33, No. 24; d, T-43, No. 38; e, T-43, No. 48; f, T-43 No. 58; g, T-33, No. 23; h, T-43, No. 23.

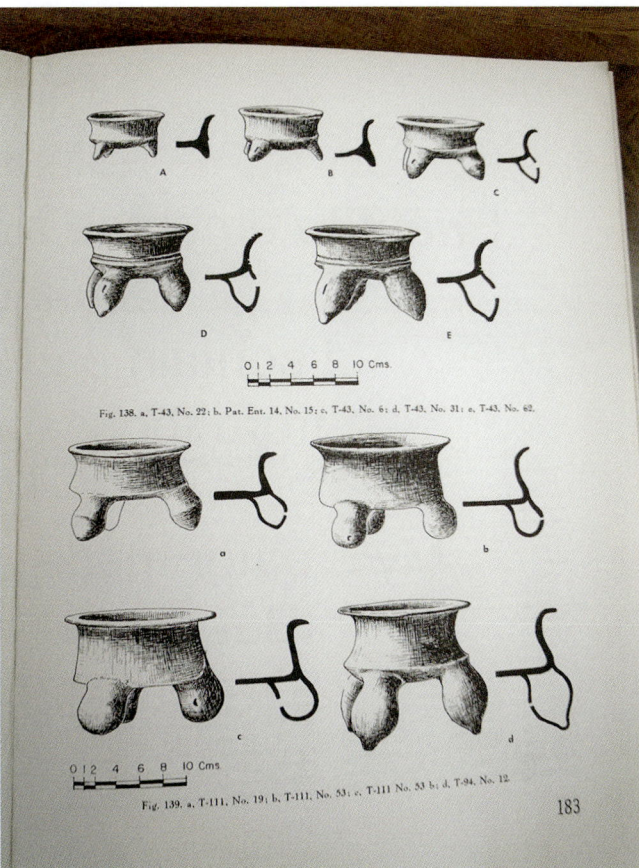

Fig. 138. a, T-43, No. 22; b, Pat. Ent. 14, No. 15; c, T-43, No. 6; d, T-43, No. 31; e, T-43, No. 62.

Fig. 139. a, T-111, No. 19; b, T-111, No. 53; c, T-111 No. 53 b; d, T-94, No. 12.

Hi again!
This is me,
plaaaaastic
I want to embrace a high resolution fantasy
I am a container
I contain parts of petrified life
from thousands of years ago

My creator made me easy to consume
But my nature is invasive—
I am a chameleon
I change everything I touch

The taxi driver who took us to Juárez International Airport on our first visit to Mexico City told us that each year in Banamex there is a plastic fair called Plastimagen. Apparently, it happens to be the biggest fair in the whole Latin America. The scale of which you only get an inkling of— is overwhelming. The human desire to produce and consume stretches like the material itself. This is where we went to look for the reasons and ask questions that nobody wanted to answer.

The fair lasts for a few days, and plastic manufacturers from all around the globe come to show their latest products including a foldable box made from a single mould, a heart valve or blood vessel made from biodegradable polymers, a thermoplastic manhole cover (unlike metal ones nobody wants to steal it from the street), or super-fast moulding machines manufactured by espresso lords somewhere in Italy. Despite the fact it is the most indebted oil company in the world, Pemex, Mexico's state-owned petroleum company, had the most elaborate stand by far.

Among this myriad of synthetic information where materialist ideology manifests to satisfy every cheap consumerist fantasy the only salvation was a green exit sign and a shot of mezcal.

What do you do
with it
when you don't know
where it starts or where it ends

The colours are vibrant,
you breathe it,
it's making you dizzy

A long line of Plastimagen visitors queue to get free brooms and baskets.

Colours, patterns, more colours,
20m wide, 1.5m long, oh a broom!
Pink, green, transparent, oh a bottle!
oh a basket!
I enchant your domestic life
I mesmerise you into delirium

We approached several recycling stands, hoping to learn about some of the advanced techniques that would make cohabitation with the material more bearable. But we left the booths only to find tiny plastic particles wrapping around our fingers and clothes like magnets. We felt like a huge plastic vortex was opening up under our feet. When asked why it becomes electromagnetic and sticky like this, we received only silent looks.

A salesman from a Chinese pigmentation company told us that although cheaper, it is difficult to sell recycled plastic in Mexico. Recycled plastics going through a production line for a second time don't usually come in bright or light colours.

Regardless of the costs, in Mexico, colour is the priority, and that has been the case since pre-Columbian times when the Aztecs were producing bright reds, yellows and blues from naturally sourced ingredients.

In contemporary societies, people always talk about the consumption of goods, as if they were actually consumed and disappeared (SMALL, E. William (1970), Third Pollution, New York, Praeger Publishers). Yet we may ask: who has actually consumed a can of beer, or construction rods, a car, food packaging or yesterday's newspaper? No one, no human being has ever done that. In that sense, we are merely users of the products, not consumers. Modern economy is entirely based on extracting natural resources, turning them into consumable products, selling them, and then forgetting all about them[§]

The City restlessly weaves living complexity throughout the day and night. People gather in it, for the flow of energy is stronger. This energy is both constructive and destructive. The City has become a ferocious polluter of the planet, breaking natural agricultural environments, it struggles to sustain an ever growing population. Devastating poverty and lack of clean drinking water comes as no surprise, and as the norm for many cities these days. Mexico City is one such megacity that has to deal with the consequence of the global and local ecological crisis with extreme urgency.

We approached Héctor Castillo Berthier, professor at UNAM Institute for Social research, author of the extensive work *Garbage, Work and Society*. In tandem with his academic practice, he organises a community space for youth gang members, encouraging them to embrace their creative powers through art. As Castillo Berthier tells it, in the early 1980s, when he started working with the subject of garbage, the environment was neither a fashionable nor a serious problem, and environmental pollution was not considered a viable area of research within the social sciences. To open up the subject from its base he had to enrol into a participatory area of research and worked as a street sweeper and then as a garbage collector on a truck. After a few hours of talking to the professor we firmly stepped into the subject of garbage collection in Mexico City, which to this day works as a self-organised and self-regulated system owned by slum gangs and operated by scavengers, collecting trash from residents or dumps and recycling it for further use. Berthier describes this hierarchical organisation as follows: "At the top is the state infrastructure, where all the benefits it can and must provide pass through the neck of the hourglass where the *cacique*ⁱ is located. He receives them, interacts with the authorities and administers these benefits in a way that enables him to strengthen his economic and political real and virtual power. Conversely, at the bottom of the hourglass is the group comprising the majority of the scavengers."

A significant mechanism that Castillo Berthier examines through his research is the human labour around recycling systems for the solid waste that is being generated daily, and the profit circling around this service. Over the last fifty years solid waste management has developed into a market system that generates new value via reusable facilities. This mutation and cycle is being enabled by constant production and a capital intensive pressure to tailor for us, the consumers. The garbage circulation creates social and economic complexity which involves diverse social groups who are interlinked in this endless cycle of consumption and reproduction of objects, substances and value. "One could begin by saying that garbage is worthless. When it is thrown into a wastepaper basket or bin it is worth nothing, but from the moment it is collected, transported, stored, classified, cleaned, sold and reused, it is transformed into merchandise. This means its use value and initial exchange value can be recovered if human labour is incorporated. This can be expressed in the following formula:

Garbage + Labour = Merchandise, which although apparently simplistic, implies a long, complex process of economic circulation" writes Castillo Berthier.

Under the competitive realm of productivity, waste management not only generates new value, but also creates new communities around the city dump sites. Thousands of scavengers manually perform one of the foundational services for the sanitary maintenance of the city sorting out the garbage and distributing it to recycling factories that largely depend upon this labour. These communities around the world often work under the most precarious conditions; exposed to toxic environments they commit to intense labour driven by senseless free market consumerism. In Mexico these workers live without social benefits or health insurance, their homes stand next to the piles of garbage and their labour is immensely underpaid and unrecognised. Castillo Berthier writes, "These people have established a wide network of relations with other groups; and whether these relations are formal or informal, dependent or independent, aimed at subsistence or at gaining political power, they are all useful for society as a whole." Thus men, women, children and the elderly, whether through force or choice, are processing everything left behind by the creatures of the city.
This community holds the consciousness and knowledge about the sanitary management of waste. (Re)construction of the city community should begin with an acknowledgment that each citizen contributes to this complex network and environment that is exposed to the chaotic energy flows.

This image, possibly framed by acres covered with hills of trash; hundreds of pigs, cows, and donkeys feeding on waste; vultures quarrelling over the corpses of dead dogs, and semi-naked children playing with flat balls or broken old toys with a thousand swarms of buzzing flies getting into their faces; this place surrounded by stench—the stench of rotting shit that lifts with the sun at noon—is not an imaginary picture, it is the actual portrait of open-air dumpsites that scatter all over the Third World §

laumes' memory notebook:

1. We stand in front of a house and wait outside the metal gate for someone to respond to the doorbell. The pleasant voice of a woman speaks over the intercom and we open the gate that leads to the house. A huge mural of the screaming face from "In the Court of the Crimson King" from King Crimson, a famous British progressive rock band welcomes us. We speculate that this reproduction might have been made by one of the youth gang members enrolled in Héctor's community programme "The Flying Circus".

2. It is remarkably silent, almost as if the city's beat is buried under the many layers of calm Sunday streets, despite the fact we find ourselves already in Monday. We go up the stairs, an Escher drawing of endless steps morphing into a pattern in the hallway saturates Kafkaesque feelings. We reach the first floor and the secretary welcomes us with a warm smile.

3. In fact, we are half an hour late to the meeting. In return, we wait for one hour in the hallway staring at a pile of books in the nearby room. We breathe quietly, and listen to Héctor's bold voice behind the closed door. One of the city dump managers was just in his office to talk. We later exchange a hand shake with *el senior*.

4. At first, Héctor invites us to go to the room where he works on his computer. A plastic tarantula crawls on the wall, and the expression on the professor's face tells us he is deep in his thoughts. We are a bit nervous as we don't know what to ask exactly. Afraid to stir him from the metabolism of his thoughts or his previous conversation, we share a minute of silence. The electric blue light of the room doesn't make it any easier. The thin air of guilty unawareness sinks through our white but not exactly privileged bodies.

1

2

3

4

5   After a short introduction and a couple of perfunctory questions we go back to the room where Héctor was having a meeting with the boss of the scavenger community earlier. The dualism of Hector's mind is like the two rooms—split between theory and social activism to build the bridges necessary to connect diverse communities across the city. The room looks like a detective's office, or some old reception foyer loaded with bureaucratic papers. There is no order or hierarchy, rock concert flyers are present along with spreadsheets and calculation forms, together with cigarettes, a cross, and a little mariachi figurine. This chaos builds a more familiar ground for conversation, no longer made tense by the thraldom of silence. There, we noticed an artefact deriving from modern Mexican mythology, a bust of narco-saint—Jesús Malverde— who originates from the Sonoran desert area, and is believed to be an angel of the poor. According to Patricia Price, "Narcotrafickers have strategically used Malverde's image as a 'generous bandit' to spin their own images as Robin Hoods of sorts, merely stealing from rich drug-addicted gringos and giving some of their wealth back to their Sinaloa hometowns, in the form of schools, road improvements, community celebrations." As Héctor talks about his work with scavenger communities, especially the children who spend their days at the dumps without any promise of an education, social care or future, our gaze wanders around the room which in itself is a museum of wonders.

6   This image is materially missing. We walk out of Héctor's office in La Merced neighbourhood, southeast of the historical centre of Mexico City. The street is silent as before, our bodies somewhere in a sister universe. We make a turn, and stop in front of an almost Coen brotheresque cinematic scene—an empty street complete with burning wheel and a handful of kids staring at the fire. The rubber and fire theme continues.

Plastic. Mostly chosen for its easy reproducibility, low material costs and a never-ending variety of manufacturing possibilities. Having one moulding machine enables the creation of multiples, adding grains of colour means you can make it into a series.

We visited a small plastic factory owned by a family who previously sold vegetables but gradually converted their business into a mini plastic industry, because it requires less maintenance and is a popular item at the market today. During our previous visit to Héctor Castillo Berthier we learned that around 70% of Mexico's population is involved in the black market economy of which this type of mini businesses is a prime example. It provides for a community: they make 20 litre plastic bottles to distribute drinking water around the city (a daily necessity in a city of 21 million where tap water is undrinkable), employs people, provides goods for the market. All of this kind of low-value manufacturing happens under the most shady of conditions—the bottles are made from recycled plastic whose origin of raw materials is not transparent (much like the bottles themselves) and many synthetic plastics are not suitable for containing food or consumable liquids. Poor working conditions equate to modern day serfdom that many in the country would never dare to question. The music from a radio weaves through the noise of the factory machines, and we follow a delivery guy to the exit who leaves on a bicycle fully loaded with freshly pressed plastic bottles.

I am born out of a blue cocoon,
blown into transparency
I contain water like a jellyfish,
and transmute testosterone
If I touch, I bring your testosterone levels down.

The mould for a 10 litre water bottle.

Manufacture
manu factum
manos
les main
il mani
money
industry, machinery, mechanically, naturally

On our last trip to Mexico at the beginning of 2018, we wanted to return to Oaxaca where the conversation about this project took its departure. The region of Oaxaca, which is renowned for the unique beauty of its textiles and pottery, once had whole villages working in the artisanal practice. With the rapid replacement of mass production some of these traditions could not keep up with the speed of the money being printed. On our first visit to the city, in 2014, we noticed the famous plastic bags weaved from specially-produced multi-coloured plastic rods and speculated why and how they had become so popular. Especially when we saw the same bags made of palm tree fibres that looked even more impressive. It is not uncommon to find plastic materials replacing natural ones in many traditional crafts. Comically, newly produced plastic objects take their ornamental design cues from structures that were inherent to the original. It is almost as if plastic wants to possess the ancient spirit and fossilise the memory of the ancient knowledge in its elements, but its abundance and speed is overwhelming.

We got in touch with Martina Garcia Garcia, an artisan, who taught us how to weave. With our hands in conversation with one another, we let our fingers meditate upon the material, thinking and reading through its history, we gave shape to an object: an unfinished basket. Anni Alberts in her book *On Weaving* says that "Basketry is thought by some to be a direct ancestor of weaving." Although made of plastic—like a Frankenstein, if positioned in the family tree of baskets—this new object didn't have a domestic function. If turned upside down it became a hat, a carrier for thoughts instead of objects, a future ancestor that might tell a story.

"We touch things to assure ourselves of reality."
On Weaving, Ani Albers

Weaving as a form of communal meditation; a remedy against anxiety over living and loving, class struggle and belonging. Through simple gestures it mobilises the power of mythological memory—the world's primary memory of elements. It creates space for contemplation and conversation. Weaving choreographs your hands into a solid sensuous memory. It is an action that creates patterns, symbols and language in infinite way of understanding. A signal to the signified.

Martina Garcia Garcia works both in the artisanal centre of the city of Oaxaca where she sells the goods, and at home, where she weaves them and manufactures new items for export to the USA and Europe. The village where Martina lives is by the side of a highway. Many people travel by so called "group taxis", which go from one end of the highway to the other collecting passengers straight from the highway, who come from the various villages that branch off from it. The "group taxi" always seat three people in the front and four people in the back, making it very tactile, soft and warm for everybody. Literally mobilising the social and the collective, the "group taxi" users will never suffer from a crisis of socialisation. We would frequently come back to the analogy of a "pot of tamales"—be it a dance floor situation or a ride in the taxi. Once we took a ride from the local taxi company and the driver didn't want to take us beyond the highway, explaining that it would damage his car. Perhaps, it was a combination of the two of us attracting attention by arriving with a taxi to Martina's house and him driving by the dusty rubble road in fear of breaking anything in the car which belonged to the company he worked for.

Long colourful hair
seeping from deep under the sea
wrapping around the Earth
like magnetic tentacles
entangling and transforming living bodies

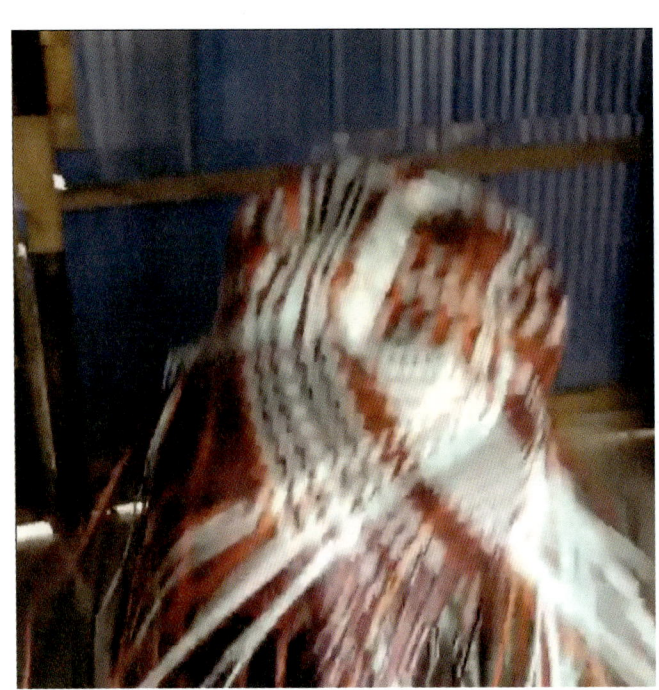

Entering into the mind or plastic to bond with the material, to hear the stories of its becoming and its vicious living, to possess its operating mechanisms and to perform a ritual in order to revert its life.

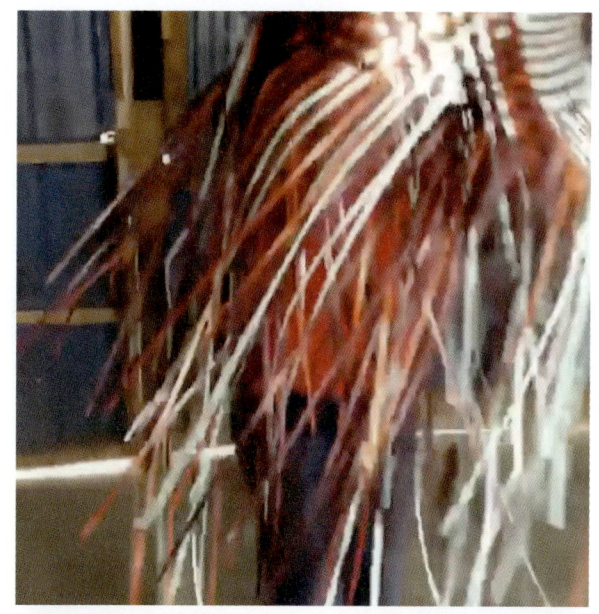

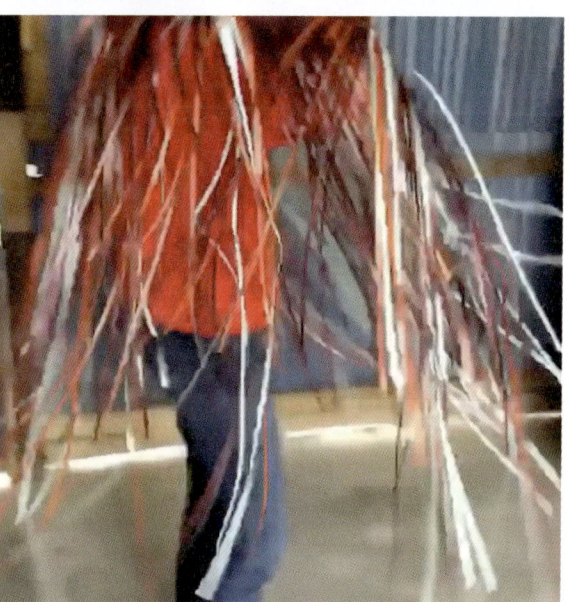

Workshop with students at the Universidad Nacional Autónoma de México in Morelia

21 Feb 2018, 14:28

My dear Bernardo!

I hope Brussels keeps catching the fires of your curiosity. Vilnius is full of snow, if you were to come here we could build an igloo with it.

My better half from *laumes* told me that you wanted to know more about the workshop that we did in UNAM Morelia. In this letter I enclose the workshop assignment and description. We created a tool that offers multifarious readings of an existing physical object that could be related to the history of plastic. As a reading tool we used a classical astrological chart dividing it into 12 groups that help you to understand the cosmic and local story that belongs to the chosen object.

We worked with both art theory and design students, and we also visited other departments on the campus just to give students a fresh idea of how other professionals conduct their research and how they work in general. So we were lucky to see the geology department that works with local volcanic rock, and we went to the biology department to see the world through their microscope that can zoom in 3000 times.

laumes itself is a collective that is closely tied to design practice in the broadest sense. Most of all of what we have been thinking about as a collective that works with educational institutions, is designing a tool for research, and therefore learning together with students and their tutors. So far our experience in Morelia was very productive and meaningful, and it would be great to extend it to other places too.

Mucho amor from Vilnius!
Viktorija

- Find a relation to the object using the chart. Fill in the chart you have received.
- Build an individual story based on information you gathered. It can be an image, text, song/sound, choreography/dance, film, etc.
- When you choose a medium be aware of its constraints. E.g. if you choose to make an image, don't forget to think of it as a tool to tell a story; if you choose to make a dance, see movement as writing and make a gesture to define your connection to the object. Make it simple, make it short.

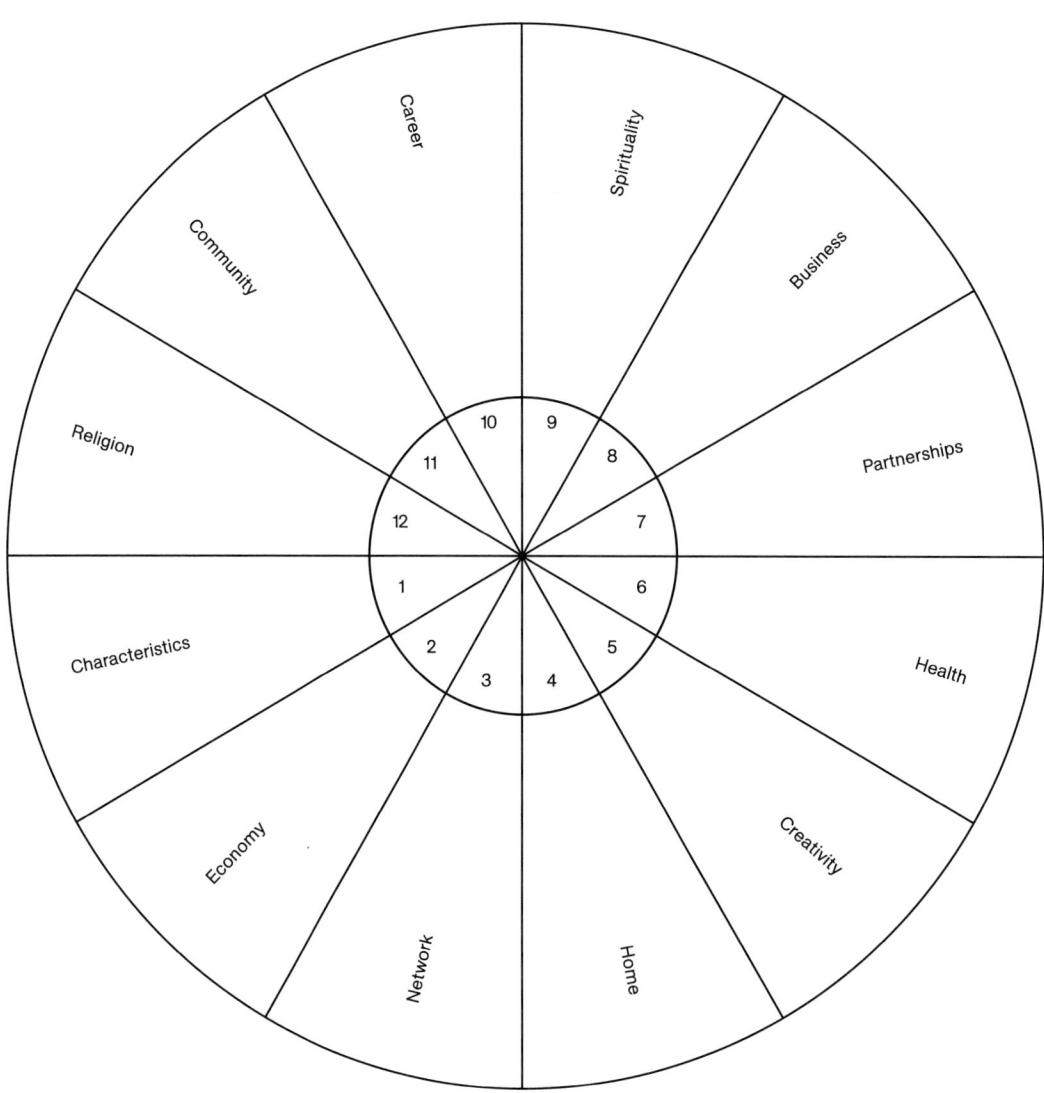

1. Characteristics: What is the shape, colour, size of the object?
2. Economy: What kind of impact or change did it bring to the market?
3. Network: How does it connect to humankind? What is the evolution process of the object? From which natural form or ancestor did the object evolve?
4. Home: What is the object's place of birth? What is the identity of the object through a given culture?
5. Creativity: How does it shape ideas and language?
6. Health: How does it interact with a physical and/or living body? Does it have an impact on health and/or well-being?
7. Partnerships: Does this object need another object to exist? E.g. cash machine/bank card. Or is it self-sufficient? Is it possible to replace those relationships with something else? Does the object have an assigned gender? Is it made for a specific gender?
8. Business: How long will this object last in the market of goods? Is it already dead? Was it replaced by something else?
9. Spirituality: How does this object influence the perception of the world? Does it it alter relationships between people?
10. Career: Where is the object positioned on the staircase of social hierarchy? How much does this object depend and/or influence social structures and hierarchies?
11. Community: Does this object produce emotional bondage? Are humans emotionally dependent on it?
    How much is this object dependent on natural resources?
12. Religion: What kind of impact does religion have on the creation or sustaining of this object?

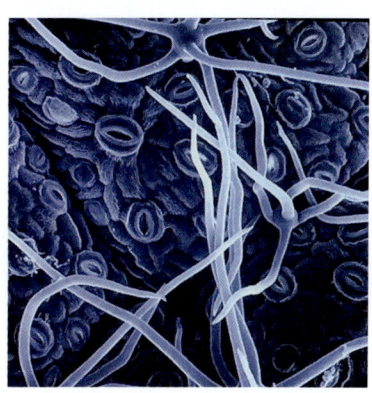

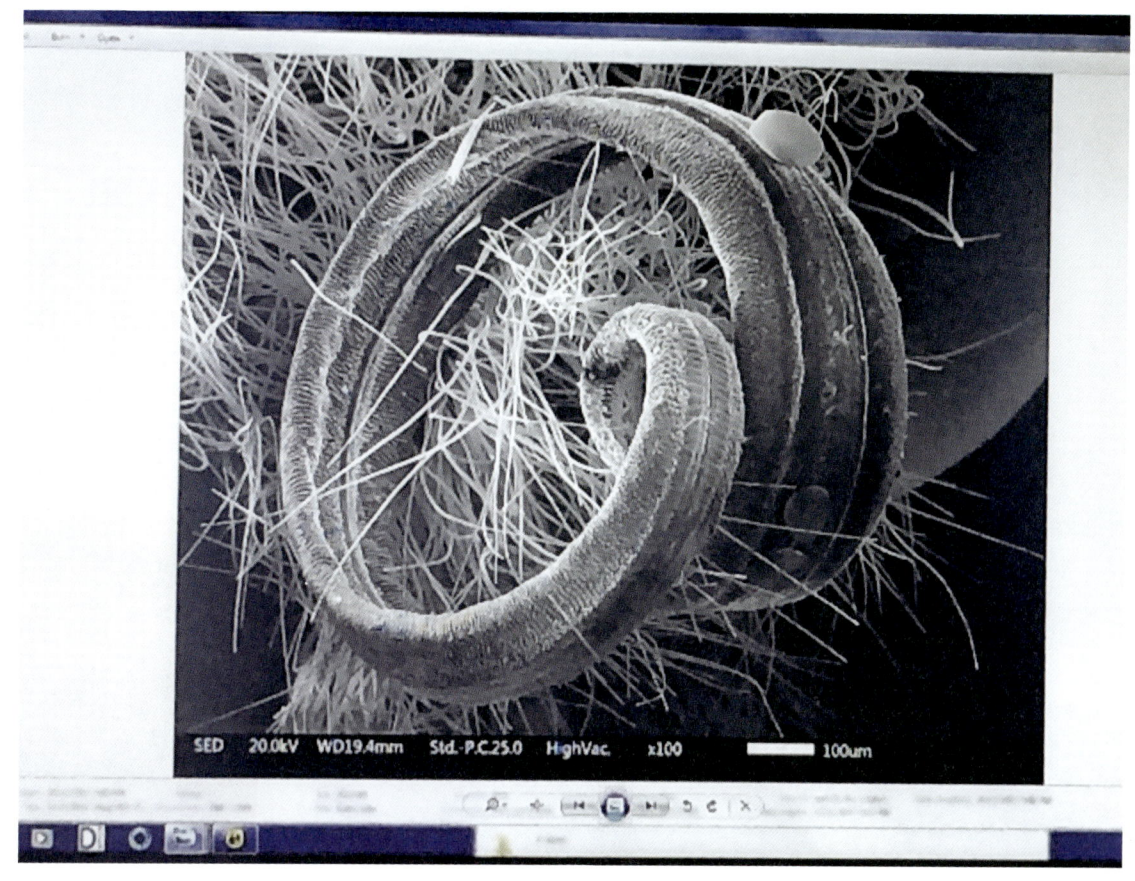

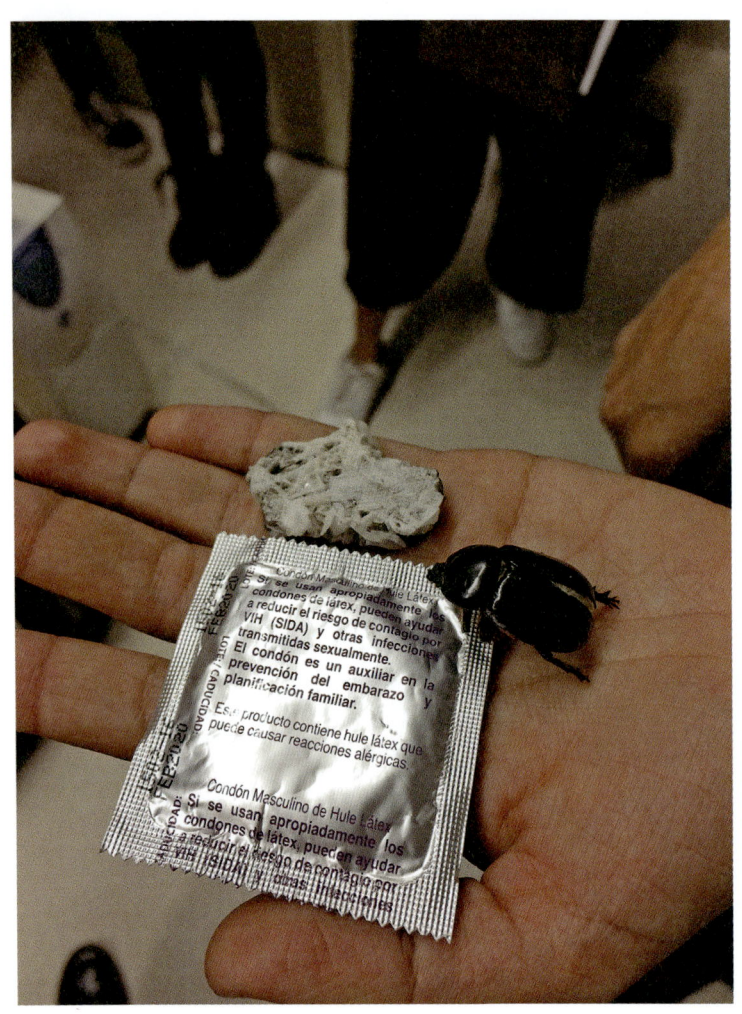
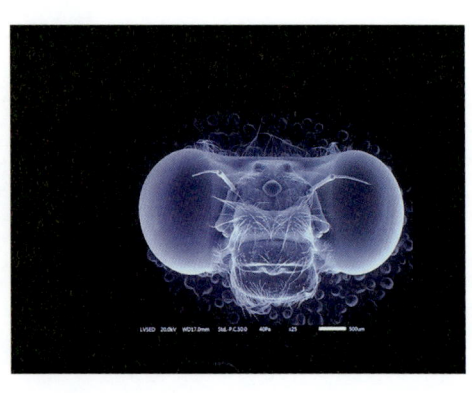

A ritual in Zipolite beach in January 2018

PEYOTE CHANT

The blue flowers.
The blue flowers
which are
behind the mountains
which are talking,
which are talking.
You
who claim to know it all,
interpret them,
interpret them.

Earth,

        Take back the broken clay pot,
                the amber
        Take back the rubber gloves,
          the morning glory flower
        Take back the plastic bag
             and the basket
      Take back the paraffin candle
          and the plastic straw
         Take back the palm leaf

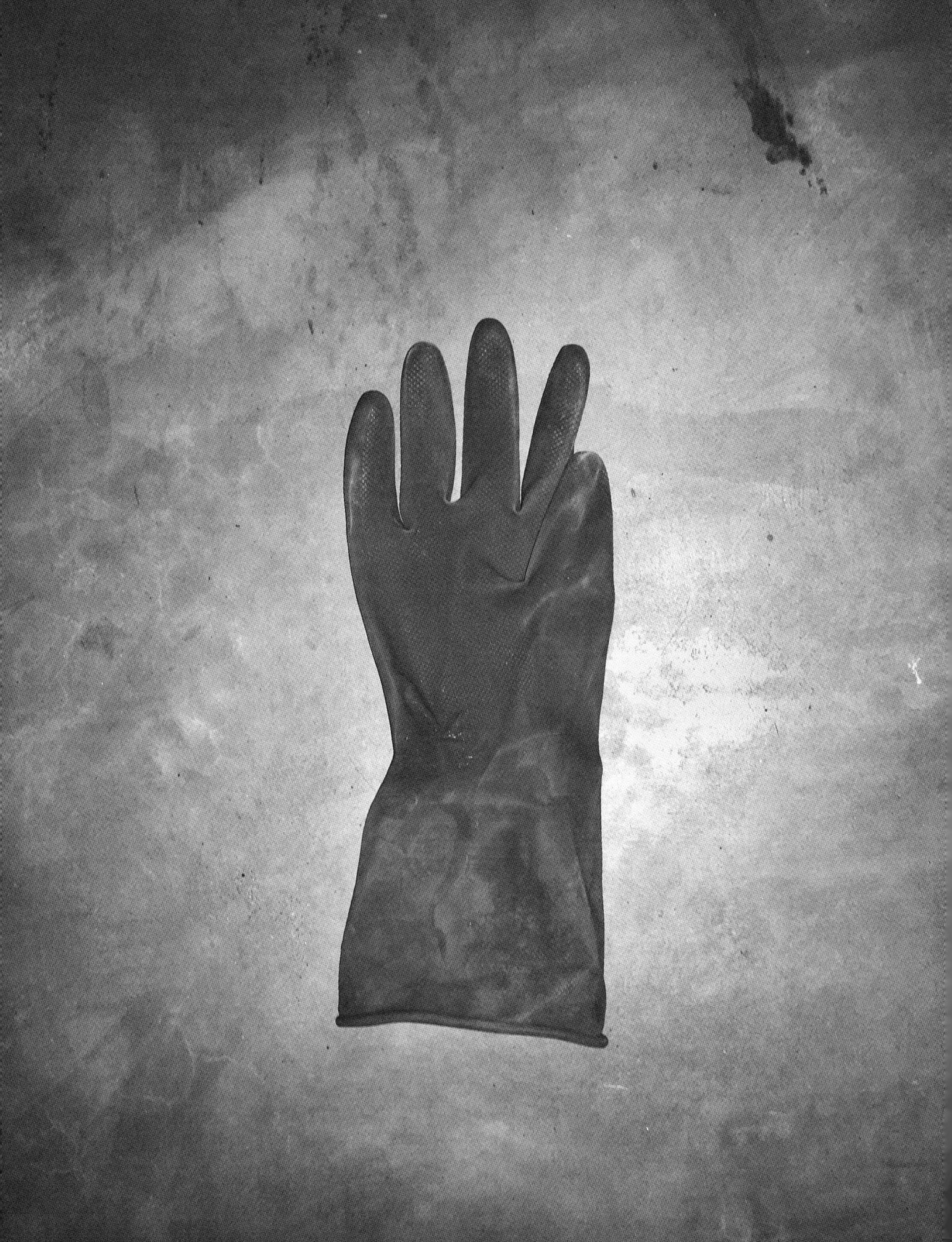

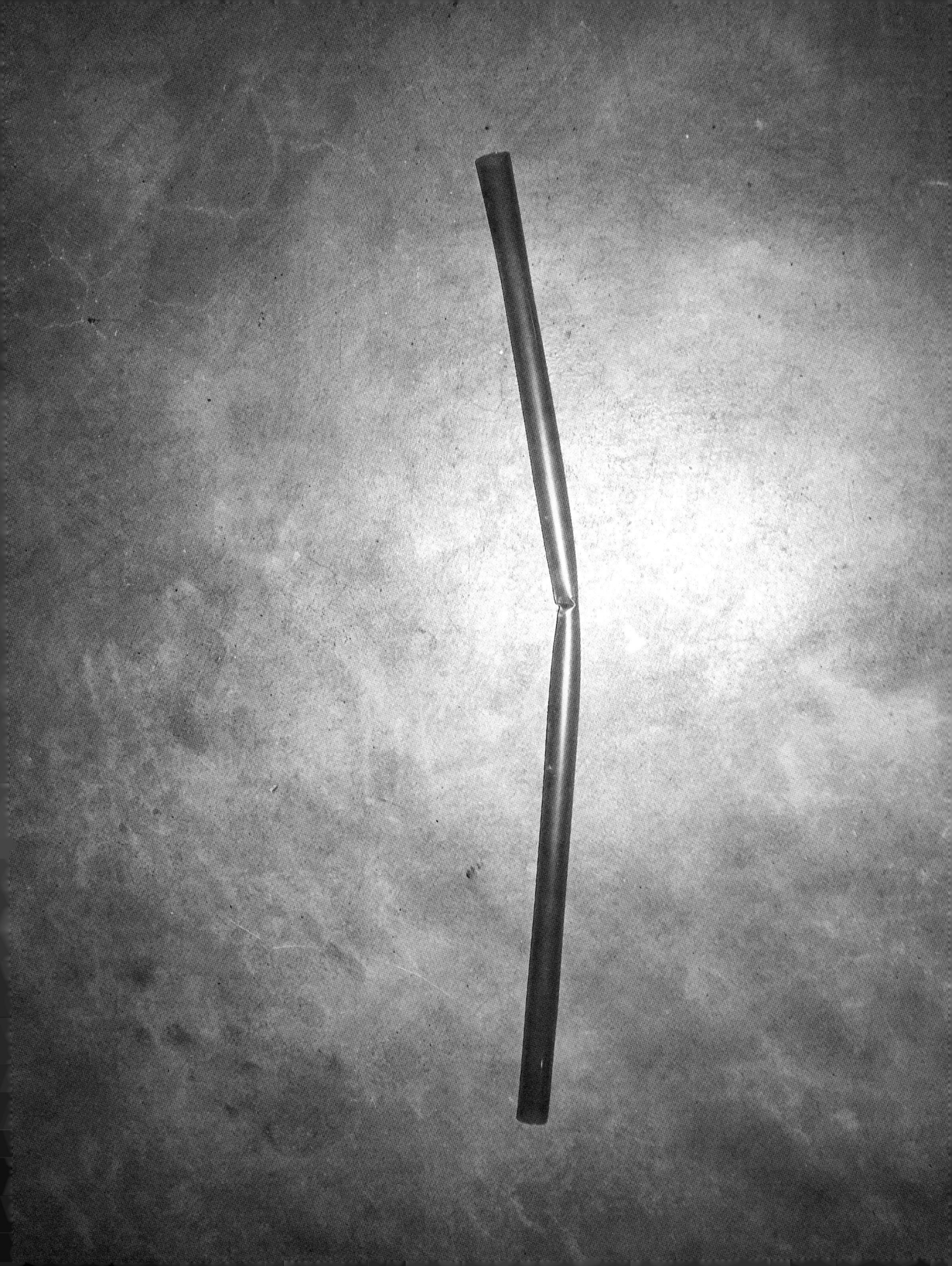

On 31st January, 2018 during a full moon eclipse we performed a ritual for and with the Earth, letting go and letting in the new energy by burning some of the main artefacts taken from our plastic timeline. It felt like a closure and a beginning at the same time.

This image summarises a history of plastic, which we unfolded over four years, and have now compressed back into a rock—returning the knowledge sprouting from the deep layers of the Earth back to the ground it came from. This fire was composed of a rock, clay, amber, morning glory flowers, rubber gloves, and a woven plastic bag—all materials that at some point shared the knowledge of plasticity in its many forms.

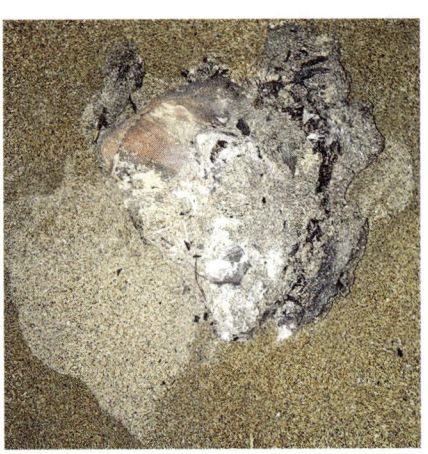

This carmine red volcanic spill might look like a rare mineral growth inside a marble block. But in reality it is just a common way of dealing with the cracks occurring in the steps of Mexico City's metro stations by cementing them with red epoxy filling. It is said that among silver and gold, the red cochineal pigment was highly treasured by Spanish colonisers who later traded it with the rest of Europe. Its special preparation process includes drying and crushing the female cochineal insect that lives mostly on cacti. Red carminic acid extracted from the insect turns it into an intense and long lasting shade of red pigment. The same red would also have been used in the pre-Hispanic illustrated codices. According to the scholars who studied the carmine red pigment road, it became a symbol of power and wealth in Catholic Europe—painters applied it to their works of art, kings used it for their upholstery, popes would wear lavish heavy red dresses to emphasise their spiritual wealth and power.

We speculated that this was derivative of the natural shellac applied on the stairs, whose preparation process also includes secreting a substance from female insects and whose colour is very similar to carmine red. But soon we learned it was not as durable as the synthetic one. Red in Mexico is still almost one of the most omnipresent colours, next to pink and azul—you eat it and you walk on it.

The Sun that lives inside the Rock
at Kunstverein München

Post Brothers
Chris Fitzpatrick

Post Brothers

At the beginning of 2018, the interdisciplinary research, production, and design studio *laumes* surreptitiously embedded themselves into Kunstverein München's history. *laumes'* permanent installation *The Sun that lives inside the Rock* operates at a scale of deep time, encompassing the entirety of the geological timeline from the beginning of the Earth to far beyond human existence. Their timeline, text, workshops, installation, and related research concern the long history and evolution of material plasticity, from igneous, sedimentary, and metamorphic rocks, clay, and amber, to natural rubber, synthetic plastics, and new polymers, all of which are currently combining to form a new geological layer made up of plastiglomerates. By repairing fractures in the art institution's distinctive granite stairs with synthetic polychromatic polymers, the pair added a new layer to the material makeup of the building and called attention not only to the stratified layers below our feet, but also to the ways materials carry memories and shape our present. This combination erodes any distinction between natural and artificial, and highlights the shaping, moulding, agglomeration, and transformation of materials across time by both human and non-human actions.

One of the inspirations for the permanent installation was the idiosyncratic way that workers often melt plastics to repair stairways and civic spaces in Mexico City and elsewhere, mending stones trodden by millions of pairs of feet by embedding recycled multicolored detritus into cracks and divots. Now, this process has been applied to the stairs of the Kunstverein, at once restoring and updating the steps and instigating an intimate reunion of sorts of rock and plastic. Curiously, this act of fallacious reparation brings attention to the human history of the steps, and all the bodies and energies that have flowed through the building. While the Hofgarten Arcades where the Kunstverein is currently located was constructed in the seventeenth century, it is unlikely that these particular slabs of stone have remained untouched. It is likewise unclear if this stairway was the same that Hitler and his cohorts ascended when the infamous *Degenerate Art Exhibition* was held in the same gallery space in 1937. Since only the roof of the building was destroyed in the bombings of Munich during the war, it could be assumed that these steps were the same when the Kunstverein, an institution that has been together since 1823, moved into the halls in the 1950s. While there was a series of renovations in the early 2000s, documentation photographs of exhibitions and events in the Kunstverein suggest that the steps have largely remained unchanged, and therefore have absorbed the impact of thousands of artists, art viewers, and other agents throughout the ages and into posterity. Yet the turbulence, treads, trauma, trials, and tribulations faced by these steps has a much longer history.

Neither a mason nor a geologist have been invited to inspect the stairs at the Kunstverein and appraise its material composition or the industrial, chemical, and geological processes that have shaped the steps. While they may look like marble or travertine—

limestone made of sediments of dead matter and minerals compressed and heated over millennia—careful scrutiny reveals that the slabs of rock are granite, the result of the progressive intrusion of plasmatic magma through layers of rock. As this aqueous melt of elements ascended the Earth's crust, it fractured the layers and grabbed rocks and minerals from its surroundings, conglomerating and cooling materials at different speeds and timescales, yielding the stone's variegated, granular, and crystalised appearance. Plastics and their essential petrochemicals similarly are a trace of movements formed through an intricate dance of liquids and solids, pressure and heat, time and concretisation. The petrochemicals distilled and synthesised in plastic production are made up of the remains of an almost unimaginable amount of organic matter, the sedimentation of the dead and all their lingering energies are "brought to life by the strings woven from the hydrocarbon corpse juice."¶

Since its expansion and omnipresence in the twentieth century, philosophers and scientists have had the tendency to regard petrochemical plastics as an emblematic sign of the modern. It is regarded as a protean substance resolutely antithetical to nature, a miraculous sign of human domination over the world through artifice. For the first time, human manufacturing was not constrained by the scarcity of nature, and instead incorporated a logic of excess. Though plastics were at first heralded for their ecological replacement of limited natural resources, we know now that their tendency is to spread, pollute, and intrude into all spaces, a result of plastic's essential excess and malleability. A prosaic and ubiquitous substance, plastic effaces its origins, grabbing molecules from abstracted substances and arranging them in impossibly new chains and relations. It masquerades as a benign, stable, smooth and malleable whole more than the sum of its parts. Yet the hydrocarbons deployed in plastic's makeup do not come from nowhere, they are things risen from the dead, reanimated and combined into anything and everything. The proliferation of plastic today is not simply a result of human auto-destruction, but a resurgence of subterranean energy brought to the surface and forming new assemblages. The past returns and is invariably re-digested by the Earth through the geological hybrid assemblages of plastiglomerates. The future effect and longevity of this material is unimaginable just as the formation of the stones is incomprehensibly distant. Inheriting this logic of historical debris and fusion, the plastiglomerate returns and reverts the chemicals and minerals to the source from whence they came.

The cracks and fissures of the Kunstverein's stairway are the result of the heterogeneity of both its stone substance and its pressures over time. By summoning melted plastic to emerge and fill these faults, *laumes* invokes the excess energy of magma and how its intrusion to the surface synthesises new elements and relations. Plastic is indeed a return to this protean logic of substance, channelling a molten core of heat to conform, transform, and adapt to different conditions like formless plasma. The multi-coloured reparations describe processes of condensation, assimilation, conglomeration, polyaddition, metamorphism, and cross-linking, and replaces the "leftovers" of the geomorphic process with a more pliable compound. The plastic embraces its craggy mould, filling the rock's cavities, rubbing a surplus of carbons together. This agglomeration yields new structures and behaviours, where extracted and synthesised elements come into contact with their ancient cousins through the latent fire of transformation within. Like the stairs themselves, the story of both plastic and rock is one of physical and symbolic ascensions and descensions. Plastic is an instantaneous adhesive that binds temporalities, an omnipresent substance that brings things together, forming something new from the past, arising again changed but the same. By setting these materials into a close exchange and laying them literally at our feet, *laumes* exposes the kinship of rocks and plastic as products of the distribution, redistribution, compression, formation, and deformation of matter imbued with energy, history, and a legacy. Where an institution like the Kunstverein thrives through the temporary movement and appearance of people and things through its history and in its present, *The Sun that lives inside the Rock* makes visible a temporality that extends far beyond our reach in both directions.

Chris Fitzpatrick

Hi, I've been all over the place, and got nowhere. Finally, I find myself slamming my VUs so I stopped here. I thought I could try writing about tape saturation in relation to plastic, and the digital emulation of analogue behaviour in relation to skeuomorphism (see, all these years later, Jonas' text still resonates with me). Vibrations, voltage, valves—pounded into a magnetic surface. Flat and fixed, but deep and encrusted in harmonic distortion. Playback adds that variable, that wobble, while a space bar just engages total recall. But I can't write.

Two questions in the cadence of Dwight Schrute: Can a dog hear AC bias? Can we still hear the difference between a tape snap and a plug in percentage?

Towards your plastic, I wonder if there's something about the fact that this is all so well encoded now—through software that not only emulates the behaviour of great valve and solid state electronics, but also operates as a black box behind a user interface that looks like the face of that very equipment, albeit also as an encoded simulation on a screen (which is, of course, electronics, which is, of course, a black box).

A Sequential Circuits Prophet 10 is on sale for $11,069.77 US dollars right now, while UVI's digital version costs $79. Meanwhile, the trade war has affected China's consumption of used American plastic. And even the most luxurious granite bathroom will make a turn towards putrid if the grout molds. There's an entire subset of the audio industry focused on replicating the analogue mistakes digital technology fixed. And there are some travertine holes filled with Milliput in Munich. That the plastic will outlast the stone is not to be held against the plastic.

Before Cher made auto-tuning infamous, engineers used to record Madonna at a slightly different tape speed. People filter their self-portraits. And while I was wandering back and forth from 440 to 432 Hz tunings, Viktorija pointed out that Hedy Lamarr was an actor who, along with a music composer, used FHSS to make missiles hop carrier frequencies within a large spectral band.

The discernible difference between the analogue and digital object, interface, and behaviour is becoming more negligible. Will future ears care? Stone/plastic—these are fake dichotomies, I guess. The plastic in the stone stairs is the plastic-stone-stairs, I guess. And the plastic must have a reflective surface, like a mouldy bathroom, and a frequency, like the stone, but is it negligible? Without your psychedelic colours, would future feet even notice? You encoded it all so smoothly. If Marconi was right, and sound never disappears and just echoes inaudibly, infinitely, then it makes me happy knowing that the plastic and the stone are sitting there— pitch-shifted projectiles, petrified in a brontosaurus with purpose—reflecting the sound of their own respective formations, of those since, and of all sounds to come (encoded, experienced, both).

PS: I was born at the peak of Disco, so I am of the Fischer Price and Casio generation. Huge gated reverbs, resonant filters, vocoders, synthesized drums, and other omnipotent toppings of the time garner much fetishization these days, but they were futurological. With a Synare 3, Ultravox slapped the abyss in 4/4, but so did Joy Division. Those tools were emulating robots that didn't yet exist. And that these robots are today being used to simulate the expressive subtleties of a world-class violinist's fingers on a $250,000 dollar Stratavarius through a $47 dollar MIDI mod wheel with near-perfect verisimilitude should not be held against the robot. Anyways, it's probably not unrelated that the current resurgence of interest in cassette tapes is driven largely by digital natives. Maybe they feel a disconnected nostalgia for a flawed technology they see as authentic. I get that. The clunkiness of fast forwarding and rewinding tape, the frustration of seeing it eaten by its machine, then spooling it with a pencil, not to mention the limitation of it being contained in and on a fixed object (a plastic cartridge), on one hand. And the warm sound of magnetic particles hissing, the spectral effect of intermodulation, phasing, artefacts, azimuth, wow and flutter—this struggle must also be part of the appeal. Like the unpredictable "woooooh-wee-oh-ooouhhhh-wooooooooo..." sound of what used to be VHS nightmares, maybe it's indeed that unmistakable warble—summoned randomly during playback, or programmed to occur in a way we'll perceive as random—that best demonstrates the elasticity of sound (other than a really good gospel singer, that is), and its plasticity. People ride horses while cars drive themselves. And people will climb your stairs, even post-stairs. Matter cannot be destroyed.

Chris

Colophon

El Plástico, the Sun that lives inside the Rock

Editors
Goda Budvytytė, Viktorija Rybakova

Authors
Goda Budvytytė, Chris Fitzpatrick, Catherine Malabou, Post Brothers, Viktorija Rybakova, Kristupas Sabolius

Copy-editing
Gemma Lloyd

Proofreading
Daragh Reeves

Graphic design
studio laumes (Goda Budvytytė, Viktorija Rybakova)

Lithography
Daniel Samulevič

Printing
Petro ofsetas, Vilnius

Edition
500

Publisher

BOM
DIA
BOA
TARDE
BOA
NOITE

Rosa-Luxemburg-Strasse 17, 10178 Berlin
www.bomdiabooks.de

Co-publisher
The Baltic Notebooks of Anthony Blunt
www.blunt.cc

ISBN 978-3-96436-020-5

The Deutsche Nationalbibliothek lists this publication in the Deutsche Nationalbibliografie; detailed bibliographic data is available at http://dnb.dnb.de.

All rights reserved, including the right of reproduction in whole or in part in any form.

© 2020, the editors, the authors, BOM DIA BOA TARDE BOA NOITE, and The Baltic Notebooks of Anthony Blunt

Image credits

Front and back cover photograph
Rasa Juškevičiūtė

p.44
https://fr.m.wikipedia.org/wiki/Fichier:Tepantitla_mural,_Ballplayer_B_Cropped.jpg

p.127, p.129, pp.132–136
Chris Fitzpatrick

All the other images, unless stated otherwise, © authors

Thanks to all of those whose conversations have helped bring different parts of this project to light; to Virginija Januškevičiūtė, Chris Fitzpatrick and Matthew Post for the invitation to exhibit; and to Sophie Nys at The St. LUCA School of Arts, Max Dossin and Chantal Garduno at the UNAM Escuela Nacional de Estudios Superiores Unidad Morelia, and Kristupas Sabolius at the Vilnius Life Science Campus in Vilnius University for the invitation to take part in seminars and workshops.

Project research supported by
Lithuanian Council for Culture, Archivo Diseño y Arquitectura, KIOSK Flanders State of the Art

Publication supported by

creative industries fund NL

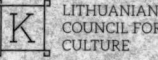

stichting
Niemeijer
Fonds

LITHUANIAN COUNCIL FOR CULTURE

Colophon

TITLE: to the Sun that has voiced the flock

Editing
Chloe Hryvnycho/Хлоя Гривнякова

Author
Gleb Gryvnychyi/Гліб Гривничий
Sofronius Malakos, Past Brothers
Viktoria Prolisoks/Олег Сак-Себастіна

Copy editing
Gemma Lloyd

Proofreading
Danija Beraa

Graphic design
Aliona Turpce /Ілона Будуйчук,
Viktoria Tyvakova/

Lithography
Daniel Sam level

Printing
Petro, Kaunas, Vilnius

Edition
800

Publishers

DOM
DIA
BOA
TADE
BOA
NOTE

Bogenberg Mount street 11, 10179 Berlin
www.bogenberg.verlag

Co-publisher
The Bally's XO pounds of Anthony Stern
via a subject cc

ISBN 978-3-96436-002-5

The Deutsche Nationalbibliothek
lists this publication in the Deutschen
Nationalbibliografie; detailed bibliographic
data is available at http://dnb.dnb.de.

All rights reserved, including the right of
reproduction in whole or in part in any
form.

© 2020, the artists, the authors, DOM DIA,
BOA TADE BOA NOTE and The Bally's
XO pounds of Anthony Stern

Image credits

Front and book cover photograph
Kasia Nevoluna

p.64
Source: ru.wikipedia.org/wiki/
Michael Poeddin, in: al. Bachyev
BLOCopper.jpg

pp.xi, a-220, pp. 125-129
Chris Chappellas

All the work images unless stated
otherwise are © authors.

Thanks to all of those whose conversations
have helped bring to fruition parts of this
project. In light of Violanta Tanska, Adrina
V... Archive and Martynav Prot for the
publication exhibit and to Sophia Tyre at
The BRICKA Scholar of Arts M.E. Bodin,
and Orchid Gardens in the UMAA Scholar,
Russian designer Una Suvorova, United
Motala, and Xanange Studio at the
Vilnius Chemistry Cluster in Vilnius
University for the invitation. Thanks to all
seminars and workshops.

Project research supported by
Eurasia Cooperation Culture Archive
based y Anatomycha, KroSE Flanders
Sites of Brava.

Publication supported by

creative industries fund NL

Stichting
Fonds